Celebrate Literacy:
The Joy of Reading
and Writing

by Jerry L. Johns, Susan J. Davis, June E. Barnhart, James H. Moss, and Thomas E. Wheat

 Education Information Press

in cooperation with

 Clearinghouse on Reading and Communication Skills

Co-Published 1992 by:
EDINFO Press
Carl B. Smith, Director
Smith Research Center, Suite 150
2805 East 10th Street
Indiana University
Bloomington, Indiana 47408-2698
in cooperation with
ERIC Clearinghouse on Reading and Communication Skills
Carl B. Smith, Director

ERIC (an acronym for Educational Resources Information Center) is a national network of 16 clearinghouses, each of which is responsible for building the ERIC database by identifying and abstracting various educational resources, including research reports, curriculum guides, conference papers, journal articles, and government reports. The Clearinghouse on Reading and Communication Skills (ERIC/RCS) collects educational information specifically related to reading, English, journalism, speech, and theater at all levels. ERIC/RCS also covers interdisciplinary areas, such as media studies, reading and writing technology, mass communication, language arts, critical thinking, literature, and many aspects of literacy.

TRIED is an acronym for Teaching Resources in the ERIC Database.

This publication was prepared with funding from the Office of Educational Research and Improvement, U.S. Department of Education, under contract no. RI88062001. Contractors undertaking such projects under government sponsorship are encouraged to express freely their judgment in professional and technical matters. Points of view or opinions, however, do not necessarily represent the official view or opinions of the Office of Educational Research and Improvement.

Acknowledgments: Cover concept by Lauren Gottlieb.

Library of Congress Cataloging-in-Publication Data

Jerry L. Johns...(*et al.*)
Celebrate Literacy: The Joy of Reading and Writing
(Teaching resources in the ERIC database (TRIED) series)
Includes bibliographical references.

1. Reading (Elementary)—United States—Handbooks, manuals, etc.
2. Language arts—United States—Handbooks, manuals, etc.
3. Teaching—Aids and devices—Handbooks, manuals etc.
I. Johns, Jerry L. II. Series
LB1537.C434   1991   372.6'044'0973—dc20   92-10630   CIP

ISBN-0-927516-30-6

Table of Contents

Series Introduction

Dear Teacher,

In this age of the information explosion, we can easily feel overwhelmed by the enormous quantity of material available to us. This is certainly true in the field of education. Theories and techniques (both new and recycled) compete for our attention daily. Yet the information piling up on our desks and in our minds is often useless precisely because of its large volume. How do we begin to sort out the bits and pieces that are interesting and useful to us?

The TRIED series can help. This series of teaching resources taps the rich collection of instructional techniques collected in the ERIC database. Focusing on specific topics and grade levels, these lesson outlines have been condensed and reorganized from their original sources to offer you a wide but manageable range of practical teaching suggestions, useful ideas, and classroom techniques. We encourage you to use the citations to refer to the sources in the ERIC database for more comprehensive presentations of the material outlined here.

Besides its role in developing the ERIC database, the ERIC Clearinghouse on Reading and Communication Skills is responsible for synthesizing and analyzing selected information from the database and making it available in printed form. To this end we have developed the TRIED series. The name TRIED reflects the fact that these ideas have been tried by other teachers and are here shared with you for your consideration. We hope that these teaching supplements will also serve as a guide or introduction to, or reacquaintance with, the ERIC system and the wealth of material available in this information age.

Carl B. Smith, Director
ERIC Clearinghouse on
Reading and Communication Skills

USER'S GUIDE *for*
Celebrate Literacy:
The Joy of Reading and Writing

These lessons offer practical suggestions for you to help your elementary-school students discover the fun involved in becoming and being literate. The authors—all of them experienced professional experts in the teaching of reading and writing—recommend following "the pleasure principle" in communicating the joy of reading and writing to youthful literates. We do best what we most enjoy; what we do not enjoy, we have trouble learning.

This TRIED volume results from an effort to *integrate* instruction in the language arts.

- There is a section on strategies and skills, but there is also a section on literature.

- Ways to become a "published" author are recommended throughout, even for the youngest writers.

- Computer literacy is as important in our time as learning to use a quill or pencil was in the past.

- "Frames of mind" being what they are, literacy learning needs to be supported by learning through music, acting, sports, and other activities that appeal to frames of mind other than the literate.

Above all, reading and writing are fun and games for minds. Let it be!

LESSON DESIGN

These lessons offer ideas that were first tried and tested in the classroom environment, and then reported in the ERIC database. The ED numbers for sources in *Resources in Education* (RIE) are included to enable you to go directly to microfiche collections for the complete text, or to order the complete document from the ERIC Document Reproduction Service (EDRS). The citations to journal articles are from the *Current Index to Journals in Education*, and these articles can be acquired most economically from library collections or through interlibrary loan.

Beginning with resources found in the ERIC database, these lessons have been redesigned in a consistent format for your convenience. Each lesson includes the following sections:

Source (your reference to the original in the ERIC database)

Brief Description

Objective

Procedures

Personal Observation

space for your own **Notes/Comments**

The lessons are addressed to you, the teacher. In many instances, the TRIED text also addresses your students directly. These directions to the students are bulleted "•". Read these instructions to your students, or revise them, as you prefer.

You know your students better than anyone else does. Adapt these lessons, taking into account the ability levels present in your classroom. Some of the lessons were specifically written for certain levels, but they can be easily modified. Think of these lessons as recommendations from your colleagues who TRIED them and found that they worked well. Try them yourself, improve on them where you can, and trust your students to respond with enthusiasm.

Activities Chart

	Reading Skills	Oral Language Skills	Silent Reading	Parent Involvement	Probe Questions	Writing Skills	Drama	Newspapers	Student Book Selection	Games	Cloze Procedures	Spelling & Grammar	Poetry
Classroom Reading Strategies and Skills													
Read Whatever You Like (p. 2)	X												
Good Reading is More than Basic Skills (p. 4)	X	X	X	X									
Experience Charts (p. 6)	X			X									
Reading with ELVES (p. 8)		X		X	X	X	X						
Our Own Library: The Critic's Card (p. 10)	X				X				X				
Locked Closet Book Collection (p. 13)									X				
What's on Your Mind? (p. 14)					X								
Partner Reading (p. 17)	X					X							
Flexible Grouping (p. 19)	X												
Synonym and Antonym Cloze (p. 20)	X										X		
Scratch-it and Zip-off Cloze (p. 22)											X		
Read-aloud Cloze Procedure (p. 23)		X									X		
Multiple-Choice Cloze (p. 25)											X	X	
Ready, Set, Read—and Reflect (p. 27)	X		X		X								
Reading Is About Literature													
Discover Storytelling (p. 31)		X											
Fill in the Poetic Blanks (p. 33)													X
Rediscovering Fairy Tales (p. 34)						X							
Scrambled Poetry (p. 36)	X												X
Reading with the Folk (p. 38)		X				X							
On the Air with Poetry (p. 40)					X		X						X

Activities Chart (continued)

	Reading Skills	Oral Language Skills	Silent Reading	Parent Involvement	Probe Questions	Writing Skills	Drama	Newspapers	Student Book Selection	Games	Cloze Procedures	Spelling & Grammar	Poetry
Reading and Other Media													
Computer Pals (p. 43)						X							X
Making Reading and Writing Visual (p. 45)	X	X				X							
Coaxing the Reluctant Reader (p. 48)	X	X											
Reader's Theater (p. 50)	X					X	X		X				
Read and Act (p. 52)	X					X							
Reading Fun and Games													
Making Progress in the Sport of Reading (p. 55)	X												
Book Mobile Book Reports (p. 57)					X	X			X				
Monstrous Reading (p. 59)						X							
Read All about It! (p. 61)								X					
Growing a Bookstalk (p. 63)	X												
Howdy, Partner! An Old-West Classroom (p. 65)	X						X						
Reading Parties													
Principal on the Roof (p. 68)				X									
Parents as Partners (p. 70)				X						X			
A Story Party (p. 73)										X			
Friday Night Prime Time (p. 74)				X			X			X			
Books and Birthdays (p. 76)										X			
Adopt-a-Book: Phase One (p. 77)		X											
Adopt-a-Book: Phase Two (p. 79)						X	X						
Battle of the Books (p. 81)	X			X		X			X				

Introduction

Am I a Literacy Celebrity?

Source

ED 298 462

Ediger, Marlow. "Reading and the Learner (A Collection of Essays)." 1988.

As you celebrate literacy with your students, keep the following questions in mind as a self-test of your own attitude towards your students' reading. If you can say yes to all of these questions, then you're a literacy celebrity!

1. Am I facilitating success and enjoyment by guiding each student to read what he or she, at his or her own level of ability and expression of interest, will enjoy reading?

2. Am I fostering satisfaction and a sense of achievement by guiding each student to read to his or her highest potential?

3. Am I providing a plethora of reading materials—accommodating every student's (ever-increasing) level of reading ability, meeting every student's interests, probing into areas of discovery for every student?

4. Am I helping my students exercise their intellects with the same joy that they sense when the coach guides them in the exercise of their bodies?

5. Am I affirming their reading choices, even when I myself would not choose to read what they selected?

6. Am I going to the trouble to help those students who are not having fun reading to start having fun reading?

7. Am I helping them attain the skills they need to make reading easier and therefore more pleasurable?

8. Am I being effective at guiding their taste in reading towards intelligence and maturity?

9. Am I diagnosing their reading levels and reading difficulties accurately? If not, what do I need to know about reading instruction that I do not know?

10. Am I devising enough different learning activities so that students with different frames of mind, learning styles, and other individual differences can make the most of their reading?

11. Am I using assessment measures that arise from the reading that my students most enjoy, so that their high interest and satisfaction can help them show off at test time?

12. Am I objective enough about my teaching to look squarely at the causes of failure in my students who do not achieve the desired objectives? Can I learn from their mistakes what my mistakes are? Am I teacher enough to correct these mistakes for the sake of the incoming class?

Comment

This book is about making reading and writing fun for your students. Being literate is something to celebrate because it is an entirely satisfying accomplishment.

"Nothing succeeds like success," they say, and that goes for reading, too. If your students are succeeding at reading, then they are naturally enjoying their reading. When you help them succeed at reading by encouraging them to read what they like to read, then you are using the Pleasure Principle to guarantee their success as readers. Reading for information, reading because one is "supposed to," reading for self-improvement, reading to meet one's needs, and reading for all those other heavy-duty adult reasons, can come later. In this book, we *celebrate* reading, and that means we have fun.

Classroom Reading Strategies and Skills

Classroom Reading Strategies and Skills

Read Whatever You Like

Source

ED 236 595

Motivational Strategies for Teaching Language Arts: A Resource, K-12. Atlanta: Georgia State Department of Education, 1982.

Brief Description

Students have an opportunity to read materials that are outside the traditional school curriculum and that have a high interest correlate with students' interests.

Objective

To incorporate high-interest topics into the school curriculum that will offer students appealing reading materials that match their achievement levels. The use of high-interest materials with students fosters an interest in independent reading and reading for personal enjoyment.

Procedure

Explain to your students that reading material may come from all kinds of sources other than the traditional textbooks found in their school, and that valuable information as well as personal enjoyment may result from reading materials that they themselves choose.

An outstanding list of 155 alternative reading materials is listed in Dewey Chambers and Heath Lowry's book entitled *The Language Arts: A Pragmatic Approach,* published by William C. Brown Co. The alternative materials, listed in alphabetical order, begin with #1 *Advertisements* and conclude with #155 *Zoo Signs.* You can probably add your own alternative materials to the list.

After discussing with your students the various alternative reading materials listed, try some of the following activities:

1. Direct students to select one or more reading materials from the alternative sources list each week, and have them share the knowledge gained from their personal reading.

   This activity can be repeated weekly until most of the topics have been examined.

2. Have your students think of other alternative reading materials to add to the list.

3. Have your students make a list of realistic alternative reading materials that they could refer to as a reference source for various subject areas in their school work.

Comments/Notes:

Observation

By encouraging students to become aware of the value of reading materials outside of the typical school-curriculum textbook, you will be truly illustrating your support of the concept that learning to read can be a most enjoyable goal for your students.

Student often claim that they are "bored" by school. A teacher who fosters independent reading has found one effective cure to student boredom.

Classroom Reading Strategies and Skills

Good Reading Is More Than Basic Skills

Source

ED 260 377

Newcastle, Helen and Barbara Ward. "Enriching the Classroom Reading Program." Paper presented at the Annual Meeting of the Far West Regional Conference of the International Reading Association, March 7-9, 1985.

Brief Description

Students are encouraged to develop a life-long interest in reading, and to improve their appreciation of literature beyond the basic-skills program.

Objective

To motivate and foster positive reading habits among students in elementary schools.

Procedure

Use this activity to enrich your class reading program and to foster your students' love of reading.

Motivate your students' interest to choose their own reading material.

A rule of thumb is to have 3-to-5 books and other printed materials per student, or approximately 100-150 references that may be changed monthly. You and some other teachers could exchange material so that all of you could keep your reading selections fresh. Sources may include books, newspapers, magazines, and audio-visual materials. Students almost invariably prefer paperback books to hardbound. Set aside time for your students to share what they have read with each other, and to discuss ideas that have been meaningful to them from the material read.

1. Read orally to your students.

    Your reading orally to your students will have a powerful impact on their literature appreciation you are a role model. Select appropriate topics to read that parallel hobbies and interests of many of your students.

2. Make time for uninterrupted silent reading.

    Be sure to provide at least 15 minutes of quiet reading time three-to-four times a week for this activity. Help your students select materials that are at a level of difficulty with which each student feels comfortable in reading silently.

3. Interpretation and sharing of activities related to reading.

   Designate an area in your classroom where the students can undertake creative activities related to their reading. This area could be used for displays, puppet plays, storytelling, art activities, creative writing, and the like. By providing this "special place," you are calling your students' attention to "rewards" available when the reading is finished.

4. Parent involvement in the reading program.

   Involve your students' parents in serving as adult-reader role models, both in the classroom and at home. Discuss with them their involvement in the school reading program. They can act as catalysts of reading enjoyment by bringing books and their children together.

Comment

The most important element in the student's development of a love of reading is the enthusiasm of the teacher. Walk into any classroom, and you can tell whether the teacher really respects the reading of books by how the students read.

Observation

Daniel Fader, author of *Hooked on Books*, stated that one-half of college graduates holding a bachelor's degree never read a book after leaving college. If this statement is accurate, or even nearly accurate, then we as teachers of elementary, junior-high, and secondary-level students, have a major unmet responsibility in fostering our students' life-long love of reading.

Comments/Notes:

Classroom Reading Strategies and Skills

Experience Charts

Source

ED 298 462

Ediger, Marlow. "Reading and the Learner (A Collection of Essays)." 1988.

Brief Description

Using experience charts with primary-grade children.

Objective

To provide emerging literacy experiences for primary-grade children through the use of experience charts.

Procedure

Arrange an experience in common for your students: Take them on a class excursion. Show a filmstrip or film, pictures or slides. Engage them in a class discussion. As your students share their experience orally, print what each student says on a large sheet of paper.

When each has had the opportunity of talking about his or her experience, and you have completed the chart, the students read the story with your assistance. Point to words and phrases as they are being read by the students.

After the first reading, ask your students if they want to change anything. If so, make the changes. When this process is completed, make individual copies of the chart for your students using primary type. Ask them to take their chart home to read to three different people. Have the listeners sign the student's copy of the chart. "Publish" these works by posting original copies of the charts around the classroom for later reading by your students.

Comments

The following factors support the use of experience charts:

Students become actively involved in experiences that provide them content for an experience chart.

With your assistance, students read text of their own composition pertaining to their own experiences.

Students will eventually note the connection between abstract letters being used to represent their ideas.

The content is familiar because it relates to students' own experiences.

Experience charts further students' interest in reading.

Each student becomes involved in presenting content for the group-experience chart. This group effort primes them to move into their own individual experience stories.

Comments/Notes:

Reading with ELVES

Source

EJ 396 382

Levesque, Jeri. "ELVES: A Read-Aloud Strategy to Develop Listening Comprehension." *The Reading Teacher* v43 n1 October, 1989, pp. 93-94.

Brief Description

Students are asked to build listening skills as a means to motivate and excite their interest in independent reading.

Objective

To stimulate primary-age children's interest in learning to read for personal enjoyment.

Procedure

ELVES (Excite, Listen, Visualize, Extend, Savor) is a read-aloud activity that can be used by teachers or parents of young children to increase their awareness of their own past experiences. As a tool of learning, ELVES prompts young listeners to anticipate what may happen in unknown settings. Assist students in developing this ability by having them participate in five listening activities that develop from any story or text of your choice.

The following example is presented within the context of Carolyn Lesser's book *The Goodnight Circle* (Harcourt Brace Jovanovich, 1984).

Excite

Discuss appropriate experiences that your listeners might have had associated with the story, and ask them to share their experiences.

- Do all animals sleep at the same time at night? Look at the title and picture on the book cover. What do you think will happen in the story?

Listen

Have your listeners take part during the oral reading of the story.

- Raise your hand when you hear me read something that proves you were right when we discussed the story earlier and predicted what would happen.

Visualize

Help your listeners construct visual images while listening to the story.

- Tell me how big you think the mother raccoon is in the story? Show me with your hands. Tell me what the pond looks like. How big is it?

Extend

Encourage your listeners to use the information learned from the story as a "predictor" of future situations that they might encounter.

- What did this story remind you of? What happened that you didn't think would happen? If you were the author of this story, how might you change it?

Savor

Savoring the story allows the listeners to reflect on the central meaning of the listening experience.

- Would you like to trade places with one of the animals in this story? Which animal would you be. Why did you choose that animal? Let's do a research project by using some reference books to learn more about the animal you choose.

Extension Activities

1. Ask your students to write a story based on the new information that they learn from their research investigation.

2. Have your students perform a psychodrama based on the characters in the story. Assign roles, and let the students make up dialogue and action as they go. (Because some people tend to talk more than others do, make certain that everyone has as much opportunity as they want to act out and speak their parts. Once the psychodrama is well under way, stop the action, shift the roles to other actors, and continue. Stop, switch, and restart the action as long as interest remains high. Allow everyone to have the fun of being the character they want to be.

Our Own Library: The Critic's Card

Source

ED 298 462

Ediger, Marlow. "Reading and the Learner (A Collection of Essays)." 1988.

Brief Description

Use a classroom library to encourage independent reading and share ideas for evaluating that reading.

Objective

To provide suggestions on setting up a classroom library. To provide ways for evaluating independent reading.

Procedure

Classroom libraries ought to include books on diverse reading levels and on various stimulating topics. Set up a location away from the main traffic lanes, and arrange the books under appropriate headings such as animals, sports, people, etc. The books for the classroom library may be secured from several sources: borrowed from the school library or the public library, or obtained from children's book clubs, individual students, used book stores, and garage sales. Books authored by students may be added to the collection.

Have your students develop a book critic's card file for the library. After reading a book, each student will fill out a card about the book including such information as what the book is about and whether they liked it or not. The student signs the card. As other students read the book, they may choose to discuss the book with others who have read it and filled out cards. Sample Critic's Card:

What is the book about? _____

_____

_____

Why did you like (or dislike) the book? _____

_____

Critic's signature _____

On the other side of the card, make space for other students to register their critical approval or disapproval in agreement or disagreement with the critic.

I agree ❑   disagree ❑   because _____
_____
_____

I agree ❑   disagree ❑   because _____
_____
_____

I agree ❑   disagree ❑   because _____
_____
_____

If several students read the same books, you may need several Critic's Cards.

The Critics' Circle

Develop a sense of common literate awareness by fostering a critics' circle.

1. Put a set of critics' cards in the classroom library with open-ended, generic questions to which your students respond.

2. Hold a conference with a group of students who have all read the same book. Try some of these questions:

- What does the title have to do with the story?

- What was the story about?

- Why did you select the book?

- Did you enjoy the book? Why or why not?

- Could this have been a true story?

- What were the characters like?

- Did you like (dislike) them? Are you like them?

- Would you want the character to be your best friend? Why or why not?

- Would you act in the same way that the character did?

- Were you surprised at the ending of the story?

- Could the story have a different ending?

- Would you tell a friend about this book?

- Was the book too easy, too hard, or just right?

- What words in the book did you not know?

- Would you like to read another book like this one?

3. You can use similar questions for conferences with individual students.

4. Your students might invent their own approach to sharing their enjoyment of books they read. For example, they could build a diorama, perform a dramatization, or design a mural.

Comments/Notes:

Locked Closet Book Collection

Brief Description

During either an assigned or free reading period, students are invited to select books from the locked closet. The contents are carefully shrouded in mystery, and may be taken from the closet (or chest) only when you unlock the door (or lid).

Objective

To arouse the interest of reluctant readers. To give students the personal reward and satisfaction of reading a whole book.

Procedure

Assemble the locked-closet (or chest) book collection as follows:

Choose titles from lists of favorite books often read at your students' grade level.

Have no more than five copies of any one title.

Put only paperback books in the closet.

Read all the books in the closet yourself before giving them to your students.

Begin with a small number of books, and add a few new titles each year.

Keep the records simple by posting a single sign-up sheet on the inside of the closet door or chest lid.

Encourage discussion and sharing of books with other students who have read them. For example, have students pair up with students who have read the same book to compare favorite passages.

Comments

Be sure to keep the collection under lock and key in order to foment intrigue and mystery. Unlock it only when students request it, and allow students freely to choose from among the treasure trove of books.

Source

ED 308 482

Long, Gail. "Celebrating the National Reading Initiative." Sacramento: California State Department of Education, 1989.

Classroom Reading Strategies and Skills
What's on Your Mind?

Source

ED 263 568

Fiderer, Adele. *Language Everywhere*. National Council for Teachers of English, Urbana, Illinois, 1985.

Brief Description

When you encourage students to express "what's on their minds," they are likely to find that what's important to them is important to others, too. Self-awareness and input from others helps them focus on real experiences and develop confidence in their writing. This activity is most suitable for students in grades two to four.

Objective

To write about real experiences, and to develop confidence by sharing thoughts in a nonjudgmental atmosphere.

Procedure

For this activity, you need pencils and copies of the head silhouette (at the end of this activity).

1. Pass out a copy of the silhouette of a head to each student. Ask students to respond in phrases or sentences to the following by writing in the spaces on the head:

   - Describe some object that you have kept for years because it sparks good memories for you.

   - Describe your favorite time of the year.

   - Name something that you do well, and something that you are still learning to do.

   - Describe your favorite place to be alone.

2. Fill in a copy of the handout yourself so that you also can tell "what's on your mind."

3. Ask your students to share their responses by reading aloud in pairs or as a whole class, comparing answers.

Extension

Students can individualize their silhouettes by drawing their own profiles.

Comments

When the outlines are filled in, each student will have a record of some of the things that are important to him or her, the same kind of record that a writer fashions when writing a poem or story. This activity puts students more at ease with self-expression, and is a good warm-up for a journal-writing session or a creative writing project.

Write your ideas on the next page in the boxes in "the thinking head:"

Comments/Notes:

What's on Your Mind?

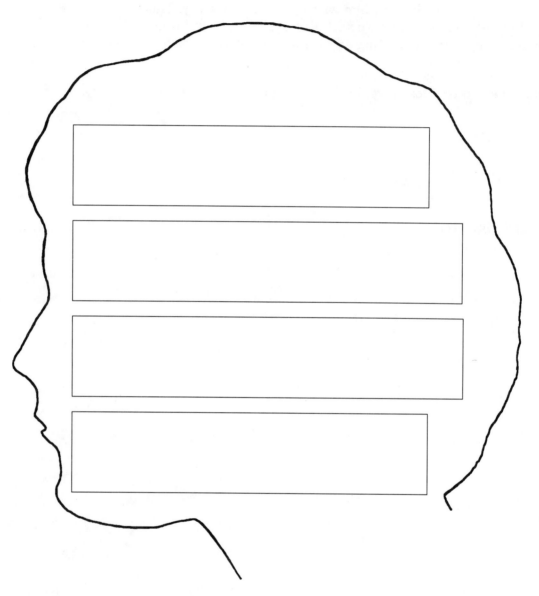

Write your ideas in the boxes in the head:

1. Describe some object that you have kept for years because it sparks good memories for you.

2. Describe your favorite time of year.

3. Name something that you do well, and something else that you are still learning to do.

4. Describe your favorite place to be alone.

Partner Reading

Brief Description

Once a week, take a break from the basal reader and let older and younger students pair up to read to each other. After they have read for a while, the younger students can dictate a story, and the older students can be scribes. Both the older and younger students can read the story.

Objective

To motivate children to read by encouraging shared reading between older and younger students. To give older students the opportunity to practice their reading and writing skills. To give younger students individual instruction and attention, and a chance to share the compositions that they are able to conceive but may lack the skills to write.

Procedure

This activity lends itself to a variety of grade levels, and is ideal when third- and fourth-graders pair up with first- and second-graders. Friday may be a good day for this activity. The entire activity covers two meetings between student pairs.

Meeting 1

Have the older students choose a book to read to their partners. Make sure that the students have practiced reading the book first. (During free time, they might practice reading with their own classmates.)

Next, have the older students read their stories to their younger partners. Send half of your students to the other room while half of the students in that class come to your room.

After the reading session, the students can talk and draw pictures about the story.

Source

Thouvenin, Anne. "You Deserve a Break," *The Reading Teacher,* October, 1989, p. 92.

Meeting 2

When students meet the second time, they can talk about the book they read together in the first meeting, and they can decide what kind of story to write. You will need to guide the older students in the process of soliciting a language-experience story. The invention of a language-experience story starts with a lively discussion. From the topic(s) in this discussion, the younger student tells the story, using his or her own language, while the older student writes it down.

Have the younger students dictate their stories to the older students who act as amanuenses. (They will like that word!)

When the story is complete, have the younger students read their stories to their partners with their partners' help as needed.

Extension

Older students can write and illustrate a poem about a character in the book. Younger students can make puppets and put on a play.

Comments/Notes:

Flexible Grouping

Brief Description

Grouping students according to shared interest is better than grouping them according to reading ability. Students with common interests, even though they have varying abilities, can tutor and motivate one another.

Objective

To afford opportunities for students to take part in, and increase motivation through, reading experiences in a variety of heterogenous ability groups.

Procedures

Group your collection of reading materials according to the interests of your students. Assign them to groups according to the subjects that they enjoy reading.

Change the groupings often so that each student belongs to several different groups and, consequently, has several group identities. Discover as full a range of your students' interests as you can so that by rearranging students from interest group to interest group, you can assume that no one settles into a rut as the best or worst reader or most knowledgeable or most bored member of a group.

Source

ED 263 519

Parker, Richard. "Towards More Nutritious Reading Programs." P.E.N. (Primary English Notes) 43. Rozelle, Australia: Primary English Teaching Association, 1984.

Observation

Students are likely to remain more highly motivated when they are not stigmatized by inflexible grouping arrangements.

Classroom Reading Strategies and Skills
Synonym and Antonym Cloze

Source

ED 263 519

Parker, Richard. "Towards More Nutritious Reading Programs." P.E.N. (Primary English Notes) 43. Rozelle, Australia: Primary English Teaching Association, 1984.

Brief Description

This lesson provides an activity using synonyms and antonyms to help students improve their system of semantic cues when reading through an aided cloze technique, making occasional use of a dictionary or thesaurus.

Objective

To develop reading strategies and promote the development of vocabulary in context by having students suggest appropriate words to fill gaps deliberately left in a given text.

To encourage students to use the dictionary and/or thesaurus when needed.

Procedure

Explain to your students the procedures involved in doing a cloze activity.

In these particular procedures, selected words are deleted from the text. A synonym or an antonym is placed in parentheses at the end of the blank. The students then use their semantic cuing system to place an appropriate word in the blank.

The following are the words one would expect in the blanks in the examples on the next page:

Synonyms

1. ordered, meal
2. glad, good
3. say/announce
4. accused
5. tired
6. costly

Antonyms

7. quickly, forgot
8. clouds
9. grew
10. new
11. dirty
12. autumn/fall

Examples:

Synonyms

1. Tom _____ (asked for) water with his _____ (food).

2. Jim was _____ (elated) when he heard the _____ (wonderful) news.

3. What did the teacher _____? (proclaim)

4. Michelle _____ (indicted) Mark of taking her pencil.

5. Chris was _____ (weary) after walking so far.

6. What is the most _____ (expensive) new car?

Antonyms

7. The waiter brought her order _____ (slowly) but _____ (remembered) her water.

8. Before it rains, we see _____ (sunshine) in the sky.

9. The flowers _____ (died) in the garden.

10. Stu has on a _____ (old) suit.

11. How did the towel get so _____ (clean)?

12. In the _____ (spring) the leaves will turn red and yellow.

Comments/Notes:

Classroom Reading Strategies and Skills
Scratch-it and Zip-off Cloze

Source

ED 263 519

Parker, Richard. "Towards More Nutritious Reading Programs," P.E.N. (Primary English Notes) 43. Rozelle, Australia: Primary English Teaching Association, 1984.

Brief Description

In this lesson, students use cloze activities to help improve their use of context as an important part of a word-recognition cuing system.

Objective

To increase reading comprehension through improved use of context by having students suggest appropriate words to fill gaps deliberately left in given text.

Procedure

Explain to students the procedures involved in using a cloze activity. Judge cloze responses on whether they convey the meaning rather than on whether they are the exact words used by the author.

The "Scratch-it Cloze" is implemented through the use of overhead transparencies on which selected words have been blotted over in the text by correction fluid. Project the sentence, and after your students have suggested what the missing words are, the blotted words can be revealed by scratching off the dried correction fluid with a coin.

The "Zip Cloze" is similar to the "Scratch-it Cloze" except that you use masking tape or post-it notes to cover the words on the transparency. The "Zip Cloze" procedure can also be used on big books or any reading material by applying self-sticking removable strips. The word chosen can be written on the strip of tape or self-sticking removable notes, and then the cover is zipped-off to reveal the word that the author used.

Observation

The "Scratch-it" and "Zip-off" procedures are highly motivating because they allow for immediate reinforcement. This technique to practice word-recognition cuing strategy proves to be much more motivating for students than does the traditional pencil-and-paper cloze technique.

Ordinary cloze exercise often are frustrating to students. By setting up their favorite, high-interest library books for use as a cloze exercise, you not only strengthen their use of context as a source of cues for meaning but also you engage them in alternative thinking: "The author said *this*, but he or she might have said *that*."

Classroom Reading Strategies and Skills

Read-aloud Cloze Procedure

Brief Description

In this lesson, you teach your students how to predict strategies.

Objective

To encourage students to make predictions about the next word, phrase, or idea when you are reading to them.

Procedure

Explain to your students that making predictions as they read is an important part of becoming proficient in reading, and that making accurate predictions will cause reading to become more meaningful, and therefore a more enjoyable experience.

Read a story aloud to your students, pausing to allow them to predict what's coming next. Ask them to justify their predictions. Discuss the possible differences between what they predict and what is in the text. Celebrate intelligent alternatives as "possibles," and do not put them down as "wrong answers."

Another approach is to have your students rough out their prediction on a piece of paper, giving them ample time for thought and writing. Afterwards, hold discussion over the various predictions.

Some examples follow:

- After Grandma stuffed the turkey, she put it in the _____.

- What word might come next?

- Why did you decide on the word "oven?"

- Grandma came out of the kitchen and said, "Dinner's ready." We all gathered and _____.

- What might the next phrase be?

- Why did you decide on the words "sat down at the table?"

Source

ED 263 519

Parker, Richard. "Towards More Nutritious Reading Programs." P.E.N. (Primary English Notes) 43. Rozelle, Australia: Primary English Teaching Association, 1984.

Observation

For at least two reasons, this strategy is a highly motivating way for students to practice predicting:

1. The material can be age-appropriate for them even if some are not reading at grade level.

2. Prediction—important reading strategy—can be practiced and transferred to the reading process by even reluctant readers through an enjoyable process, rather than through print and paper and pencil.

- The text of the story from which this example is taken reads:

  "... sat down at the dining-room table." Some of your students, however, may respond: "... sat down at the table."

- If you thought the sentence would be completed with "sat down at the table," but the author wrote "sat down at the dining-room table," what are some reasons for the difference?

- Possible answers: special meal, holiday gathering, large groups of people, some people have bigger houses—with dining-rooms—than do other people.

- Grandma put several apples, a rolling pin, flour, sugar, butter, milk, spices, and a large round metal pan on the kitchen counter.

- What might happen next?

- "Why did you decide that Grandma was going to bake an apple pie?

Comments/Notes:

Classroom Reading Strategies and Skills
Multiple-Choice Cloze

Brief Description

In this lesson, students use their semantic and syntactic cuing systems in reading in connection with a highly motivating technique that seems more like a word-game than a lesson.

Objective

To direct the reader's attention to grammar, spelling, and meaning by word-choice selections.

Procedure

Explain to the students that they can become more proficient readers by paying attention to grammar, spelling, and meaning.

Example

Source

ED 263 519

Parker, Richard. "Towards More Nutritious Reading Programs." P.E.N. (Primary English Notes) 43. Rozelle, Australia: Primary English Teaching Association, 1984.

- Circle the correct word from the three alternatives given in each group below:

I hurried myself,
- hoped
- hoping
- hopping

to arrive first, but John

drew
- ahead
- even
- behind

so that I could see him out of the corner of my
- nose.
- hearing.
- eye.

A member of our class is our
- closet.
- classmate.
- clothes.

On the wall is a
- clam
- clip
- clock

to tell what time it is.

The tornado caused lots of
- farm.
- harm.
- charm.

The
- thing
- ring
- sling

slipped right off her finger.

Once your students get the hang of this word game, they can have great fun devising three-word trick sentences for one another. Challenge them to devise different kinds of three-word sets:

❖ words that sound alike

❖ words that are spelled similarly

❖ words that have similar but different meanings

❖ and many more

Comments/Notes:

Classroom Reading Strategies and Skills
Ready, Set, Read—and Reflect

Brief Description

By using the Directed Reading Lesson teaching technique, teachers can assist students to be successful in their approach to a text, and increase their success at reading.

Objective

To provide students with directions that will enhance their chances of being successful readers of text content.

Procedures

The Directed Reading Lesson teaching technique used in a lesson format generally has three stages:

Stage One: Preparation for Reading

Classroom observation has shown that the preparation stage is often over-looked or skipped. Background discussion activities start the students thinking about certain aspects of the up-coming story or passage that will have relevance to their successful comprehension of the passage.

Ask your students direction-setting questions that may be centered on the theme of the upcoming story. Encourage students to share personal experiences that could enliven the group's background knowledge prior to the individual reading stage.

For example, this direction-setting activity could be used before your class reads a story about a woman who convinces a male companion that her job possibilities are not determined by her gender. In this example, you might ask your students these questions:

- How many of you know what you want to do after you finish school?

- How many of you have made your job choice primarily because you think of it as "man's work" or "woman's work?"

- What types of jobs do you think are almost always associated with either men or women?

Source

ED 271 741

Binkley, Marilyn R. and others. *Becoming a Nation of Readers: Implications for Teachers.* Washington, D.C.: Office of Educational Research and Improvement, 1986. (Companion to Richard Anderson, *et al., Becoming a Nation of Readers: The Report to the Commission on Reading.* Urbana, Illinois: Center for the Study of Reading, 1985. [ED 253 865]

By asking questions, attempt to guide the group to the realization that almost no reason is valid to influence career and job choices based merely on gender.

Another example of prior knowledge of a topic to be read about would be sharing personal experiences. Geographical locations other than the local environment, such as neighboring environs, states, and countries, are good examples of stage-one discussion:

- How many of you have visited a national park outside of our state?

- Has anyone visited Canada? Mexico? Europe? Some other far-away place? If so, tell us about what you saw.

By becoming aware of their own and others' prior experiences and knowledge before reading printed material associated with a topic, students will have a better understanding of the content when they become actively involved readers.

Stage Two: Individual Reading

To increase a student's silent reading success in comprehending the passage, divide it into smaller segments. Each segment may be preceded or followed by discussion, questions, or both.

Stage Three: Discussion

Many young readers and poor readers do not consistently see relationships between what they are reading and what they already know about the topic about which they are reading.

You may assist your students' understanding of the passage content by using some of the following activities:

- ❖ Ask questions that integrate several points of information found in the selection.

- ❖ Ask some questions that are "open-ended" and have no single answer, but may be interpreted from the reader's own personal viewpoint.

- ❖ Teach your students to monitor their own reading by devising questions, as they read, predicting what will follow, and comparing the observed outcomes. This activity can be easily used with almost any size class. Select a suspenseful short story that can be photocopied for each class member. Present the story to the group and ask them to cover it with another sheet of paper. Have them cover the story paragraph by paragraph as they read.

The two basic questions are these:

- What is the story about?

- What do you think is going to happen next?

The other question is a harder one:

- Why? What is the evidence for your supposition about what will happen next?

Lead the discussion through the story paragraph by paragraph to the end. The major purpose is to foster interest in the story as well as to provide students with a technique to improve their own comprehension as they read independently.

Observation

When young readers feel successful, they like reading better, and they read more.

Comments/Notes:

Reading Is about Literature

Reading Is about Literature
Discover Storytelling

Source

Roney, R. Craig. "Back to Basics with Storytelling," *The Reading Teacher* v42, March, 1989, pp. 520-523.

Brief Description

Students develop competence in reading and writing skills through a variety of storytelling activities.

Objective

To motivate students to read and write. To use their expertise in speech to help them develop reading and writing skills. To develop in young students an awareness of the types of narrative literature. To augment students' general knowledge and concepts of the world.

Procedure

Most young students have mastered the basic oral aspects of their native language by the time they enter school. Storytelling taps into this expertise and facilitates continued growth in reading and writing. Here are some ideas for putting your oral experts to work:

❖ Conduct a storytelling demonstration by engaging students jointly in concocting an oral story by using language patterns provided in Martin's *Brown Bear, Brown Bear, What Do You See?* (1983). Suggest that the storytellers write and illustrate their own text by using new colors and new animal characters.

❖ For younger students, read a story such as Carle's *The Very Hungry Caterpillar* (1969). Afterwards, have the students read the printed text independently or retell it orally, using illustrations. Or, they can devise oral or written variations of Carle's text by using the syntactic structure: "On Monday he ate through one apple, but he was still hungry. On Tuesday he ate through two pears, but he was still hungry...." By substituting their favorite foods, the students can rewrite their own version of the book.

❖ For older students, you can tell fables as part of a social-studies unit on values clarification. Students listen to fables and then discuss the issues raised in such classic morals as "Liars are not believed, even when they do tell the truth" or "Slow and steady wins the race." Students can

❖ analyze the fable as a genre of literature to discover its basic plot and character format. Encourage them to compose their own oral or written versions of fables.

❖ Tell the story of *Mrs. Jones and the Vacuum Cleaner* (O'Brien, 1971) to upper elementary-grade students to help them conceptualize the meaning of the term "rat race." Then they can write their own stories to personalize and exemplify this concept.

❖ Use the flannel board to tell Tolstoi's *Great Big Enormous Turnip* (1968). Then your students can retell the tale while manipulating the flannel characters.

Comments

Storytelling builds background experience and helps students develop imagination and the ability to think inventively. You can capitalize even further on the power of storytelling by providing them with an opportunity to engage in the literature of storytelling with their other "frames of mind." Use art to involve those who are dominantly visual, and drama to involve those who are dominantly spacial, in their frames of mind. Storytelling, reading, and writing, belong to the literate frame of mind, and they need to be translated into other activities for students whose minds organize the world in different ways.

Comments/Notes:

Reading Is about Literature
Fill In the Poetic Blanks

Brief Description

Students improve their writing skills through parallel writing of poetry.

Objective

To motivate remedial writers to improve their writing through the rewriting of poetry.

Procedure

The students are given a poem, the structure and rhyme is outlined, then they are encouraged to write their own version. This activity allows students to write independently, but the patterns and structures, the idea, rhythm, and rhyme pattern into which they can insert their own ideas are all provided so that they are free to achieve a satisfying product.

Source

Wicklund, LaDonna K. "Shared Poetry: A Whole Language Experience Adapted for Remedial Readers," *Reading Teacher* v42 n7 March 1989, p478-81.

Based on "Sally and Manda" by Alice B. Campbell

_____ and _____ are two _____(Who or what are they?)

Who _____ (How do they eat?) _____(What or how or where do they eat?)

They live _____(Where do they live?)

And _____ (How do they move?) _____(What else do they do?)

Two examples of third-grade students' poems:

Till and Will are two little chicks
Who gobble up worms using lots of tricks.
They live by a haystack near a shack
And flutter all around getting a snack.

Shocker and Stocker are two electric eels
Who shock killer sharks using their tails.
They live in a pirate ship, roaming all around
And swim faster than the speed of sound.

Students can extend their writing further by making individual or class books of their poems using the repetitive patterns in the poems.

Reading Is about Literature
Rediscovering Fairy Tales

Source

ED 308 482

Ekstein, Jean & Patti Shelley. "Celebrating the National Reading Initiative." Sacramento: California State Department of Education, 1989.

Brief Description

Fairy tales contain wishes, dreams, and problems that are common to human beings the world over. Classic fairy tales from around the world come alive for students when they use them as stimuli for writing.

Objective

To promote students' original writings. To encourage them to write their own fairy tales. To develop inventive imitations. To give students the opportunity to learn about the structure of a story, to identify problems, and to see how problems are solved. To provide a picture of other cultures and other people. To enjoy the contributions of classmates.

Procedure

To use fairy tales as a stimulus for writing, you may follow this plan:

❖ Make available a rich collection of fairy tales from many countries.

❖ Make time to read aloud to your class, as well as time for the students to read the fairy tales on their own.

❖ Make time to discuss the stories, talking about the introduction, plot, and conclusion.

❖ Using a story as a model, encourage your students to weave variations into the plot, characters, and events, and then to write a story on their own. Encourage them to illustrate their stories.

❖ Give your students time to share their compositions by reading their fairy tales to the class or to a partner.

❖ "Publish" your students' work either by displaying the stories or by using your school's desktop publishing software to make a small book of original fairy tales.

Observation

Fairy tales give students a chance to visit the lands of enchantment, witches, giants, and fairies around the world. Because children of all ages love fairy tales, they can serve as an excellent springboard for a writing activity. Published in home-grown booklet form, your students' collection of original fairy tales makes an excellent opportunity to involve parents in the school's reading and writing activities.

Comments/Notes:

Reading Is about Literature
Scrambled Poetry

Source

Wicklund, LaDonna K. "Shared Poetry: A Whole Language Experience Adapted for Remedial Readers," *Reading Teacher* v42 n7 March 1989, pp. 478-81.

Brief Description

Students improve and expand their sight vocabulary through the use of poetry.

Objective

To learn to recognize instantly the words that make up a poem.

Procedure

Select a poem appropriate for the age, interests, and experiences of your students. Prepare a set of color-coded word cards for the poem: Each word is written on a separate card, and all the words of each stanza are written on cards of the same color. The students arrange themselves with partners, and together they unscramble the stanza they have been given. Each set of partners unscrambles their stanza while referring to memory or a master copy of the poem which may be displayed in the room. During this process, students will use word recognition strategies, such as matching words, and by attending to sound-symbol associations while reading the words again and again to attain the flow of the language.

After sequencing the cards, the students read their stanza and exchange word cards with others; then the process begins again with a different stanza.

This lesson includes sight vocabulary practice in context with time on task, repetition, and high motivation.

For additional repetition of vocabulary, the word cards for the poem can be mixed into a pile in random order and the students can quiz each other.

For the final activity, give each student an envelope with a copy of the poem on the outside and with word cards inside. The students take the envelopes home and share the process with their parents. The following day, the students can add all new, known words to their word bank.

A poem by Christina Rosetti

Who has seen the wind?
Neither I nor you.
But when the leaves hang trembling,
The wind is passing through.

Who has seen the wind?
Neither you nor I.
But when the trees bow down their heads,
The wind is passing by.

Comments/Notes:

Reading Is about Literature
Reading with the Folk

Source

ED 230 899

Canon, Mavis. "Folk Literature: A Motivating Force in Learning to Read." In *Comprehending Cultural Awareness and Reading*, pp. 39-40. Proceedings of the 12th Annual Reading Conference, Terre Haute, Indiana, June, 1982.

Brief Description

By using high-quality folk literature as a discussion tool in the home and the classroom, parents and teachers can motivate young children from an early age to want to read for their own personal enjoyment.

Objective

To instill in young children a desire to gain the necessary skills to explore stories of interest on their own by learning to read independently.

Procedure

1. As a parent or teacher, increase your own knowledge of children's literature. Traditional literature includes all kinds of stories, riddles, fables, myths, and legends that derived originally from the oral tradition.

Three excellent sources for your reference are *The Read-Aloud Handbook* (1989) by Jim Trelease, *Classics to Read Aloud to Your Children* (1984) by William F. Russell, and *Reading for the Love of It* (1986) by Michelle Landsberg.

2. Folktales can be organized in many different ways for oral presentation to students.

Categorization of folktales by country. The Grimm Brothers are famous for having collected and rewritten German folktales, but many other collectors have made many other collections of tales. Illustrated volumes help stimulate interest in listeners and readers to learn more about the countries and cultures of the folktales' origins.

a. *Folktales by "type" and "motif."* Folktale scholars refer to folktale types and motifs. The standard, well-known stories occur in many versions from land to land, and the bits and pieces of storytelling ("types" and "motifs") get traded around considerably.

Stith Thompson, *Motif Index of Folk Literature* (revised and enlarged), Bloomington, Indiana, I.U. Press, 1955-58.

Antti Amatus Aarne. *The Types of the Folktale: A Classification and Bibliography,* Helsinki: Suomalainen Tiedeakatemia 1964, 1973. (Translated and enlarged by Stith Thompson.)

Folk tales by theme. Standard themes include the eventual triumph of love and kindness over evil and cruelty, security *versus* fear, and the cleverness of the younger child (with whom the reader/listener identifies). High-interest themes for children include tales about animals that combine wonder and realism.

Extension Activity

Have your students select folk tales that follow a theme of their own choosing. Students could then share with the class orally or in writing their personal impression of various folktales that illustrate a particular conclusion, or they could compare two or more folktales concerning a common theme.

Folktale-telling is an excellent way to turn your classroom into a multicultural happening. Invite your students of Anglo-European descent, African descent, Asian descent, or Latin-American heritage to find and "collect" folktales from their ethnic background, write them down and then tell or read them to the class, or act them out.

Comments/Notes:

Reading Is about Literature

On the Air with Poetry

Source

EJ 343 582

Kirk, Robert N. "Tape Recording Poetry," *The Reading Teacher* v40 n2 November, 1986 pp. 200-02.

Brief Description

You can teach poetry to students at any grade level without making them dislike it. Children are natural poets; they love nonsense sounds and rhyme, and they play with words and meanings just as adults do. The use of student teams and tape recorders to increase appreciation of poetry can be an alternative to direct instruction of poetry by the teacher.

Objective

To use teams of students as an avenue to increase their appreciation of poetry without direct teaching by the classroom teacher.

Procedure

1. Ask your students of any grade or ability level to become actively involved in the study of poetry. Establish teams to select poetry that they think will be effective for oral presentation to a guest audience in the form of an audio tape.

2. Establish teams of students to preview poems that have a variety of subject matter, moods, styles, lengths, and oral approaches.

3. Have each team develop a chart with columns and headings such as Author, Title, Source Book and Page, Length, Mood, and Possibilities for Oral Presentation. Each team can review 40 or 50 poems, making a final selection of poems to be included in the tape of 50 to 60 minutes.

4. If, say, five teams are organized in your class of students, each committee can be responsible for the production of 10-to-15 minutes' worth of material. The production of each team's segment will be the result of a lot of practice taping, editing, listening to their own voices, and committee discussion.

Your role during all of the activities is to probe, ask questions, offer suggestions, and be a resource to the teams.

- Does this poem lend itself to sound effects?

- Could music be included to increase the mood of the poem?

- Does this poem lend itself better to a choral or individual presentation?

When the teams have completed their several investigations, followed by their final selections, the entire class meets to decide exactly what will go into the final tape. A student producer and student production team are selected to orchestrate the final recording.

When the tape is finished, your class will enjoy sharing their work with other classes and other audiences.

Observation

Often, poetry is viewed by students as boring and dull. Creative approaches to teaching poetry can reverse students' negative and uninformed attitudes.

Extension Activities

Your class might also want to develop a program guide for listeners, to accompany the final tape.

The program guide might include any of the following: table of contents, lines from the poems, background information about the poets, and explanation of why these poems were selected.

This tape and its accompanying program guide would make an excellent commemorative gift from your class to the school library.

Comments/Notes:

Reading and Other Media

Reading and Other Media

Computer Pals

Brief Description

Students develop their reading and writing skills by using computers.

Objective

To introduce students to the use of computers as a means of developing their communication skills within an authentic context.

Procedure

Explain to your students that the computer can be a powerful tool to increase their language, reading, and writing. Tell them that they will be given the opportunity to correspond with other students, whom they do not know, with the aid of the computer. Your students can conduct computerized correspondence in a numbr of ways, depending on your school's hardware:

1) More and more schools are going on-line with capacities for electronic mail (E-mail) via Bitnet, Internet, Telnet, and other electronic networks. If your school is plugged in electronically, your students can communicate directly with their electronic pen pals as soon as you and/or the computer teacher get them up-to-speed using the communication protocol.

2) You can simulate E-mail in the following way: Have your students key their messages into computers, download their files onto a disk, then mail or otherwise transfer the disk to the target destination. The pals at the other school can then respond to the electronic messages addressed to them on the disk, write their own messages, and return the disk to your students. Virtual E-mail!

3) If all else fails, your students can at least gain valuable hands-on experience and increase their computer literacy merely by using wordprocessing software to write ordinary letters to their computer pals. They key their messages into the computer, print them out, and mail or otherwise transfer paper copy.

You will need to make contact with an appropriate school to establish a connection so that your students and those students can correspond.

In order to initiate the project successfully, the corresponding school needs a computer and printer for the students' use. You and the other teacher work out a plan to mail student correspondence to one another every so often.

Source

EJ 388 489

Beazley, Malcolm R. "Reading for a Real Reason: Computer Pals across the World," *Journal of Reading* v32 n7 April, 1989 pp. 598-605.

Observation

The use of correspondence between pen pals has long been an established activity in our schools. Computers update this traditional activity as an extension of students' curiosity about the new electronic medium.

After each student has been matched with a peer from the other school, the following correspondence activities may get underway:

- Write a letter to introduce yourself. Use the computer to introduce yourself to your Computer Pal. Tell him/her about your interests, family, school, and the like.

- Go into detail about a topic alluded to in your first letter. Choose a topic that you included in the first letter to your Computer Pal, and explain it more thoroughly to your new friend.

- Write a fictional story or poem, which could be sparked by seasonal activities or activities occurring at school. Write a story or develop a poem which you think your Computer Pal would enjoy sharing with his/her friends. Try to use interesting words to express yourself.

- Become a journalist and write interesting articles about current events in the community and your school. Choose a topic about your school or community to investigate, and write your findings to your Computer Pal.

- Choose a topic associated with a social issue to write about. Pick a topic that is interesting to both you and your Computer Pal. You now know your Computer Pal quite well. Choose a topic we have discussed in our class and write about it to your Computer Pal. Perhaps your Pal will want to share his/her thoughts and feelings with you on the subject after reading your letter.

"The use of computers as tools in the language classroom reveals exciting possibilities for enhancing reading enjoyment and competency, particularly when the word processor and modem are utilized." (Czerniejewski, 1988)

Extension Activities

1. Use the computer for peer student writing activities beyond local school-district boundaries by arranging Computer Pals in other States and foreign countries as well.

2. Use the computer for students interested in learning the foreign languages of their Computer Pals.

3. Foreign-language learning software is available for purchase. Arrange communication exchange between students with handicaps such as impaired hearing and sight.

Reading and Other Media
Making Reading and Writing Visual

Brief Description

Presents ideas that foster development of reading and writing skills as a prerequisite for audio-visual presentations generated by students.

Objective

To encourage student presentations to audiences with the help of visual aids after preparatory reading and writing activities have been undertaken.

Procedure

Tell your students that they are going to make presentations of information to an audience on a subject of their choice. They are to use visual aids as a way to illustrate their topic, the content of which they will derive by reading and writing to document their findings.

You may foster the reading/writing/visual media connection in a number of interesting ways.

1. Oral Booktalks

   You may stimulate your students by giving a brief oral/written presentation to promote interest and curiosity in a book. Later, students can be encouraged to write and read booktalks which could be stored on computer diskettes and audio tapes for peer reference. After some booktalk practice, and reviewing their own tapes, students might share their booktalks with larger audiences.

2. Picture Booktalks

   If your school is lacking in audiovisual equipment, construction paper can be a valuable substitute to prepare a picture about the book. The procedure allows students both to share their picture booktalks directly with each other and to display their artistry in their classroom or in the library area.

Source

EJ 374 775

Sacco, Margret T. The Reading/ Writing/Media Connection. *The ALAN Review* v15 n3 Spring 1988 pp. 18-19.

3. Multi-Media Booktalks

Help your students illustrate their booktalks by using a camera to make prints/slides from pictures in books or magazines. Synchronized audio tapes of their booktalks with background music can set a mood conducive to readers' enjoyment. The activity could be an individual or class project. The multi-media booktalks could be stored in the school library for other students' use.

4. Videotape Activities

When your students videotape their booktalks, invite them to dress like the characters in their books. By playing the role of their characters, they can give first-person narratives. Another motivational technique to encourage reading is to develop a resource file of tapes of respected community adults who volunteer to talk about their favorite books before a camera. Your school could build a reference archive of all your "famous" (and not-so-famous) citizens talking about their favorite books.

5. Writing News Articles

Promote reading and writing among your students by having them read a book and write a short news article about it; then, you could use your desktop publishing software to publish your class's "Literary Journal." The use of publishing software would allow your class to develop a *Gazette about Books* that could be distributed to class members and other interested students and sent home to parents.

6. Displays

Make bulletin boards, posters, and annotated bibliographies available to your students as a means to promote interest in reading books.

Comments

Whatever techniques you have to use to motivate student reading habits, your students need to be able to check books out and take them home. Public libraries are the best source, of course, but the people in your community would be delighted to donate books for student use. Give your students, parents, and their neighbors a chance to get involved in building a special "Student-Use Library" in your classroom.

To reclaim the romance of the word, and spawn a generation of readers and writers, teachers and librarians need to work together to replace the dreary "book report" with exciting projects that involve students in reading and writing activities using computer technology and various other new media.

Be inventive! Sit down with yourself and brainstorm as many new and unheard-of ideas as you can to promote the—no matter how wild and crazy, no matter how impractical—enjoyment of reading. Write down *everything* that comes to mind. Now, look at your list and pick one or two ideas that might be doable.

Comments/Notes:

Reading and Other Media
Coaxing the Reluctant Reader

Source

ED 304 665

Rasinski, Timothy V.
"Inertia: An Important
Consideration for
Reading Motivation."
Ohio: A classroom
teacher's guide,1989.

Brief Description

This lesson increases student motivation to learn to read and read to learn.

Objective

To involve students in the act of reading by providing activities that motivate the reluctant reader to move from a passive state to an active state.

Procedures

The following activities are effective with passive students who lack the motivation to read.

Read Aloud

For students who have difficulty in starting a book, read the first chapter orally to them. Follow the oral reading by asking questions that can be used as a guide for their own further reading.

Choose a recreational book of particularly high interest. Read it aloud to your students to a point of major interest or excitement in the story. Next have a student complete the book or story by reading the rest of the book and then telling the rest of the story to the whole class.

Experience Followed By Reading

Arrange for experiences related to topics that can be further investigated in books. Guest speakers, experiments, demonstrations, skits, and artifact collections are examples.

You can use TV to foster reading in several ways. Show a video as background information on a topic before your students read a book.

Books As an Impetus

Help your students make connections between their specific interests and the books that match those interests. Assign a student who likes automobiles to read books about cars. A book about the life of Henry Ford and the development of Ford Motor Company might come next. After that, a book about car racing, foreign cars or automobile safety. You could even assign your car fanatic to read the Driver's License Manual for your state. Any reading is good reading, and one book leads to another.

Assign everyone in class to watch some especially meaningful show on TV, and then have them read follow-up books on the subject in preparation for class discussion.

Daily Time for Sustained Reading

Set aside 10 to 30 minutes so that your students may read quietly each day (or, at least, every other day) for personal enjoyment.

Offer advice, if they need or want it, and make lots of suggestions of many good books; then let your students make their own choices of what to read.

Observation

Enjoyable experiences with books lead to greater enjoyment of books. Bodies in motion tend to remain in motion. Your job is to break the inertia of your non-readers, and get them going with books. We do what we like, what feels good, what we enjoy. Get them started by letting them read for the sheer fun of it.

Comments/Notes:

Reading and Other Media

Reader's Theater

Source

ED 308 482

Stecher, Adrienne. "Celebrating the National Reading Initiative." Sacramento: California State Department of Education, 1989.

Brief Description

As an alternative to round-robin reading, "Reader's Theater" offers every student in the class an opportunity to take part in a dramatization. Because students may be performers, stagehands, narrators, or audience members, everyone is successful in one assigned role or another.

Objective

To work as part of a group to make decisions concerning the dramatization of a text.

Procedure

1. With your students, choose a book or story (fiction works better than nonfiction, unless the nonfiction is about historical events and is written dramatically).

2. Read the selection as a class, and discuss the plot, the characters, and the events. Script dialogues from the text.

3. Encourage your students to practice reading the story alone or with a partner at school.

4. Assign parts, and distribute the script among the performers and narrator(s).

5. Arrange for the narrator(s) to describe the setting, present the scene, and otherwise introduce the background for the story.

6. Stretch the imaginations of audience members by having them picture in their minds the characters and the actions.

7. Select simple, easy-to-obtain props that can enhance the meaning and enjoyment of the story.

8. After the performance, hold discussion of the story, plot, characters, and events.

9. Repeat the performance for a variety of audiences (e.g.,parents, other classes, the whole school).

Extension Activities

Students can be encouraged to write their own scripts from material that interests them, and then a play can be staged along the lines described above.

Comments

The success of "Reader's Theater" is largely attributable to the opportunity that all students have to participate and succeed in some way. Hence, the whole class takes part in reenacting the play through a class reading of the script.

Comments/Notes:

Reading and Other Media
Read and Act

Source

ED 236 595

Motivational Strategies for Teaching Language Arts: A Resource, K-12. Atlanta: Georgia State Department of Education, 1982.

Brief Description

Students act out, or role-play, situations from a story that they have read.

Objective

To encourage students to read stories to expand their imaginations by assuming the role of various characters found in their books.

Procedure

Select a story from a book or magazine appropriate to the student's reading and interest level. Either read the story aloud to the students or have them read the passage silently.

Your students may then participate in the role playing/acting out of the story.

Mime

- Without *saying anything*, act out the part in the story.

Surprise Ending

- Act out an ending to the story different from one that the author wrote.

Are You Reading Me?

- I will write a sentence or put a group of words on a card for our actors to see in secret. The rest of us will try to guess what part of the story the actors are portraying, and we will write a one-sentence description of what we see the actors doing.

Comment

Students who are low achievers require concrete examples to reinforce learning. Role playing and acting out allows students to internalize concepts and demonstrate their understanding of written material.

Extension Activities

1. Read a story together, but role-play the expected outcome before you finish the story. Various teams of students could participate in this activity. Congratulate teams who "get it right" for their ability to second-guess the outcome; congratulate for their inventiveness the teams who come up with something different.

2. Have students role-play events that led up to a familiar literary work soon to be read. An example might be Tom's whitewashing the fence in *The Adventures of Tom Sawyer* by Mark Twain. Also, almost any fairy tale lends itself nicely to the use of this technique.

Observation

Role playing allows the learner to recognize, retell, and recall the main idea, as well as give attention to detail and sequence in a story. Acting out a story provides students with an enjoyable opportunity to bring print to life for an audience.

Comments/Notes:

Reading
Fun and Games

Making Progress in the Sport of Reading

Brief Description

The use of progress charts with at-risk students can motivate their interest in becoming better readers. Illustrations showing student successes provide a visual point of reference for the teacher and student to gauge the progress of progress.

Objective

To provide at-risk reading students with visual benchmarks to measure their development in reading achievement.

Procedure

Student effort and improvement in reading are important elements of any reading lesson. This is especially true for reading students at risk of boredom and failure who may need extrinsic rewards to increase their motivation to learn to read better.

The following suggestions are effective with students who, you sense, need concrete evidence to support their efforts in reading.

For baseball fans, construct a baseball diamond on poster board with felt markers. Set up a "balls, strikes, and runs" scoreboard on which to register a list of skills to be mastered. Independent reading can be rewarded by moving a baseball from base to base around the diamond for every book read. On the skill scoreboard, record mastery exhibited in skill areas such as sight words, increased oral reading fluency, prediction, and context cues.

You may use the baseball chart to stimulate team competition. One team may consist of members who attained specific skill development while another team may consist of members who read books independently. Each time a skill is mastered or a book is read, the team advances one base or scores a run. (If you and your students are baseball fanatics, you can work out a set of rules for a game of Reading Baseball as complicated as you can stand!)

For racing fans and car buffs, develop a chart that is a three-lane race track. Each lane represents a reading skill goal such as reading rate, vocabulary development, and number of books read. Each student drives three cars which are attached with the pins

Source

ED 298 435

Webre, Elizabeth C. "Personalized Progress Charts: An Effective Motivation for Reluctant Readers." Louisiana: A classroom teacher's guide, 1988.

around the track representing the progress of the student in the skill lane identified.

For basketball enthusiasts, develop a chart titled "Slam-dunk into Reading" and target reading goals to be scored. The goals can be new sight words learned, new books read, main ideas grasped, and word attack skills gained. After a "game" has been "played" in one of the skill areas, the student could place a construction paper basketball in the "basket." Books read outside of class are counted as free shots and get two points.

For students who are not sports-minded, you can develop a chart around an interest that they specify. One student might enjoy furnishing "My Dream Mansion." The student could cut out furniture and decorate a house as a result of progress logged in various reading skills achieved.

Farm and ranch kids might enjoy stocking their barns and corrals with the cattle of reading skills. Young enforcers of law and order might enjoy blowing away the bad guys by reading about them. The ideas are unlimited: Find out what your students are interested in, and help them design their reading and skills progress charts accordingly.

Observation

The use of progress charts may be an effective way to stir up and maintain interest in remedial reading classrooms. The charts can serve as a way to reward reluctant readers for their progress without placing them in a competitive environment. Let them measure their *own* progress, rather than being measured by someone else's!

Comments/Notes:

Reading Fun and Games
Book Mobile Book Reports

Source
ED 237 927

Bates, Ellis. "Book Reporting with Book Mobiles," *The Reading Teacher* v37, January, 1984. pp. 433-434.

Brief Description

Because most of us believe that you *can* tell a book by its cover, a dust jacket on a book often entices us to read the book. Students can be encouraged to make their book reports as attractive as book jackets. After reading a book of their choice, students devise a book-report mobile. The project is fun and suitable for students in all grades.

Objective

To motivate students to share their reading interests and writing talents.

Procedure

Ask students to save empty boxes of various sizes (cereal, cracker, cookie, etc.) that they can later bring to school. Once they have collected several boxes, they can follow these steps to make attractive book reports.

1. Let students choose a book they want to read, and then set aside class time when everyone reads.

2. Give the following directions:

- Cut strings two yards long.

- Thread string through the top of each box, knotting the string so that it doesn't pull out.

- Tape the box shut, leaving the string hanging out.

- Using glue or tape, cover the box with plain, light-colored paper.

- Make sure that the string is still hanging out at the top.

- Decorate your mobile boxes using separate sheets of paper the size of the box.

- Sketch a scene, event, or character from the book.

- Drawing can help you visualize and interpret what you've read.

- You can design a book cover using fancy lettering or stencils, if you don't want to draw.

- Do a rough copy first to plan a final design that you can transfer onto one side of the box.

3. Once the drawings are finished, have the students draft one or two paragraphs explaining their sketches. Writing gives the picture life, and it then becomes the book report. Students who have lettered a cover design can write about the people, places, or happenings in their book. They can summarize the book using the five journalistic Ws:

- Who/What is the book about?

- What happens?

- Why does it happen?

- When does it happen?

- Where does it happen?

In the final paragraph of their Book Mobile book report, students explain why someone else would also enjoy reading the book.

4. After these paragraphs are revised, edited, and proofread, have the students transfer their corrected work onto the other side of the box. They can either write on the box, or write their reports on composition paper and paste them onto the box.

5. Finally, the Book Mobiles are assembled and hung in the classroom, hall, or library where other students can see and read them.

Comments/Notes:

Reading Fun and Games
Monstrous Reading

Brief Description

Students are stimulated to use the library as a reference center to read more about monsters.

Objective

To demonstrate to students how much fun reading can be, and to introduce them to the use of the library as a resource to continue their pursuit of topics of interest.

Procedure

This activity motivates your students to use the library as a resource center by inviting them to continue their pursuit of knowledge about monsters.

Children are enthusiastic about monsters. You can broaden your base of instruction to include such monstrous subject areas as art, music, and physical education as well.

The art teacher can offer instruction in monstrous mask masking. The music teacher can lead the crowd in singing "The Monsters March in One by One," "When Monsters' Eyes Are Gleaming," and "Monster Mash." The P.E. teacher can tie into the project with games such as Monster Tag and Monster Relays.

Explain to your students that monsters will be investigated according to the following categories:

Prehistoric Monsters

Folk and Legendary Monsters

Literary, Film, and Television Monsters

Mysterious Monsters

True-Life Monsters

Space Monsters

Numerous references are available in any library on the above categories. Here are a few examples: *Dinosaurs* by Nora Sullivan; *Paul Bunyan and Other Tales* by Irwin Shapiro, *Movie Monsters*

Source

ED 255 904

Fowler, Zinita. *Monster Magic: A Reading Activities Idea Book for Use with Children. A Fun with Reading Book.* Phoenix, Arizona: Oryx Press, 1983.

Observation

The subject of monsters holds great excitement for many students. The inventive teacher can capture this enthusiasm and use it to promote students' reading enjoyment and continued use of the school's library facility. Take advantage of seasonal interests, and you can get your students to read about werewolves, vampires, witches, and goblins in preparation for their own costume-making and trick-or-treating on Halloween.

by Thomas Aylesworth, *Real Life Monsters* by Martha Dickson Allen, *Giant Animals* by Howard Smith, and *Space Wars—Worlds and Weapons* by Steven Eisler.

Secure a list of media resources such as video tapes and 16mm films which can be used to stimulate interest in each of the six monster-type categories. An excellent example of a 16mm film is *Dinosaurs, Dinosaurs, Dinosaurs*. Numerous VCR tapes are available. Two popular choices among students are *Teeny-Tiny and the Witch Woman and Other Scary Stories* and *Beauty and the Beast*, the latter an Oscar-winning movie.

Secure reference materials on each monster type being presented as a means to promote interest for further exploration.

Have students keep a record of their efforts on a "monster meter" which they keep to document their list of books read and activities undertaken.

Have students participate in creative writing activities as a result of their further readings. For example, students could be asked to write about how the troll felt in the story of the *Three Billy Goats Gruff*.

Extension Activities

Have your students do a "Monster Revue" as an activity for parents or other classes. The activities might include these:

Have a monster masquerade; students dress up like their favorite monsters.

Darken the room and tell ghost stories.

Pass around ingredients for Witch's Stew such as peeled grapes, broken pretzel sticks, soaked spaghetti, and dried corn kernels.

Invite a reporter from the local newspaper to cover the revue and write a story for the press highlighting the program.

Comments/Notes:

Reading Fun and Games
Read All about It!

Brief Description

Newspapers contain many high-interest sections relevant to students. Most newspaper articles are short, and they cover a wide variety of content without being considered "babyish," in spite of their relatively simple readability level.

Objective

To use the newspaper as a source of reading material to teach new vocabulary words.

Procedures

Discuss with your students the use of the newspaper to increase their reading vocabulary both at school within the class and at home with members of their families.

The following steps are suggested as ways to use the newspaper as a reference source for teaching students new vocabulary:

As examples, mount some newspaper ads on construction paper.

Have students bring various advertisements from newspapers found in their homes. The selection of the ad can result from discussion with parents or siblings.

Have newspapers available for students who may not have access to them at home.

Organize your students into pairs. Students alternate in identifying and defining words.

One student underlines a word that demonstrates the specific skill being reinforced, such as identifying compound words (e.g., "bookcase for sale").

The student uses the word in an original sentence to demonstrate correct word meaning.

The word and sentence can be written or dictated and, later, shared with the entire class by the pair.

The other student in the pair repeats the process with a new word.

Source

ED 236 595

Motivational Strategies for Teaching Language Arts: A Resource, K-12. Atlanta: Georgia State Department of Education, 1982.

Extension Activities

Other options for using newspapers include the following:

Cut out food pictures and classify various food types such as vegetables, fruits, cereals, meats, and dairy products.

Use ads for "show and tell."

Use the newspaper for a creative-writing exercise with your students. Have students write an article about a headline and then compare their article with the article published in the paper.

Use articles in newspapers to foster debate and dialogue between and among students.

Comments/Notes:

Growing a Bookstalk

Brief Description

Designed to build a personal bookstalk chart at home for use by students and their parents.

Objective

To draw students into the enjoyment of literacy by encouraging them to read together with their parents at home.

Procedure

A personal bookstalk chart that is jointly "cultivated" by the student and his or her parent(s) serves as a stimulus and an ongoing record of literature shared by parent and child. The chart is titled "(student's name) and the Bookstalk." Each leaf added to the stalk-chart bears the name of some excellent book.

Grow the bookstalk in this way:

1. Parents read storybooks aloud to their young children who are not yet able to read on their own. For every book read, add a leaf to the stalk.

2. As the parents and young children read books, parents cut blank leaf shapes out of paper, write the title and author of the book, and give the leaf to the child to color and add to a stalk that the parent has cut out of paper (or drawn on paper that hangs on the wall).

3. Extend the height of the stalk as more books are shared between the parents and child.

Extension:

Children who can read and write on their own, or with a parent's help, can build their own chart. They write the titles of books they have read onto leaves and add the leaves to the bookstalk.

Source

ED 308 482

Schmidt, Barbara. *Celebrating the National Reading Initiative.* Sacramento: California State Department of Education, 1989.

Comment

Parents and Children Together is a monthly audio magazine (audio cassette with booklet) for parents and children, ages 4-10, to read together. Each issue contains information and advice for parents about their children's education, and (on the other side of the tape) three read-along stories that parent and child can read together, each thereby improving his or her own literacy at the same time.

"Parents Sharing Books" is a reading program for school teachers, students, and parents to support home/school cooperation and family communication through books read together. To find out more about *Parents and Children Together* and whether the "PSB" program would work in your community, call the Family Literacy Center at Indiana University (Bloomington), 812-855-5847, or write to: Family Literacy Center, Smith Research Center, Suite 150, 2805 East 10th Street, Bloomington, Indiana 47408-2698.

Comments/Notes:

Reading Fun and Games

Howdy, Partner! An Old-West Classroom

Source

ED 263 563

Blume, Pat. "Feature Project — The Old West," *Live Wire* v1 n2 October, 1984, pp. 12-14.

Brief Description

These activities motivate students to participate in speaking, listening, writing, and reading.

Objective

To encourage students to participate in learning activities by transforming the classroom into an environment that acts as a catalyst for students' imaginative exploration.

Procedure

Inform your students that the classroom will become an "Old West" town, and that they will be the town's residents.

Students will be assigned to committees for planning, constructing, furnishing, and developing the Old West town setting. Start a discussion, invite nominations, and then hold an election so that the students may pick a name for their town.

Materials may include wood, cardboard, furniture boxes, and old clothes donated by parents.

Your role will be to oversee the construction of the small town, help planners focus and clarify their ideas, and be a liaison between the classroom and the homes.

Explain to the students that the following examples might be scenes that they could stage in the classroom:

❖ A stable: bales of straw, tools, bridles, saddles, pictures of horses.

❖ A hotel office: desk and chair, keys, registration ledger, letters, blankets, towels, wash basin.

❖ A restaurant: table, table cloth, silverware, dishes and plates, menus, boxes of food such as might have been used to cook with in the Old West: flour, eggs, corn meal (nothing microwaveable!).

❖ A mine: a stream [made of paper], pans, picks, shovels and gold and silver.

Observation

Transforming the classroom into the Old West generates endless opportunities for writing, speaking, listening, and reading in areas of math, science, social studies, literature, history, geography, music, and art.

If you and your students live near any of America's numerous historic reconstructions of 18th- and 19th-century villages and towns, a class junket to the nearby show place would be an energizing way to start your own historic construction of Old West Town.

❖ A Conestoga wagon: table covered with cloth, loops for wheels, chairs, drawn by horses—(wooden or hobby horse from home).

❖ A jail: keys, guns and holsters, wanted posters of villains, cot, a cell with bars (a big cardboard box appropriately carved).

❖ A general store: clothes line to hang, bonnets, hats, scarves, candles, food items, scale.

❖ A doctor's office: cot, bandages, sling, herbs, bottles of medicine.

❖ A one-room school: chair covered to represent pot belly stove, dunce's hat, slate, a hickory stick.

❖ A one-room cabin: cardboard-box wood stove at center, table, cot, baby's cradle, sewing box, broom, banjo or guitar, rifle, kitchen equipment.

With the completion of each setting, have students participate in the following activities:

❖ List vocabulary words that are appropriate for the setting.

❖ Select and read reference materials to increase knowledge and background about the setting in an Old West town.

❖ Write a story to depict a typical event that might have occurred in the setting.

❖ Write and present a skit to represent an event in a particular setting. Other classes and/or parents can be invited as the audience.

Comments/Notes:

Reading Parties

Reading Parties
Principal on the Roof

Source

ED 308 482

Crum, Susan S.
*Celebrating the
National Reading
Initiative.*
Sacramento:
California State
Department of
Education, 1989.

Brief Description

This planned reading activity describes an offer by an
elementary school principal to spend a whole school day on the
school's roof if the students met his challenge to read for 60,000
minutes outside their classes (635 students K-6, 10 minutes at
home every night).

Objective

To promote student reading outside of school.

Procedure

The simple procedures can be followed to put any principal on
the roof:

1. Prepare a weekly home reading form so that students can
   record the number of minutes they read at home.

2. Request the parents to sign the forms and return them to
   school each week.

3. Have students total the number of minutes per week of reading
   time each has logged.

4. Ask students to total the number of minutes that their class
   has read.

5. Record the minutes on a class chart.

6. Submit the totals to the principal's office.

7. Have the principal post the class totals on a schoolwide chart
   displayed in a prominent place in the school.

8. Ahead of time, decide with the other teachers and the principal
   on a reasonable time period during which the students are to
   try to meet the principal's challenge.

9. Encourage older students in the school who have met their
   goals to help the younger students.

10. Arrange to have a desk, telephone, and other necessities on the roof so that the principal can continue his or her work for the designated day.

11. Coordinate times with other teachers so that different classes can see the principal at work on the roof.

Comments/Notes:

Reading Parties

Parents as Partners

Source

ED 308 482

Goldberg, N. Jerome. "Be Enthusiastic about Reading"; Speyer, Anne V., Pittsfield, Massachusetts; Teaching Staff of Coyle Avenue Elementary School, Carmichael, California; Stanislaus Reading Council, Stanislaus, California *Celebrating the National Reading Initiative.* Sacramento: California State Department of Education, 1989.

Brief Description

Researchers who have studied the effects of parental involvement on learning generally agree that parents contribute significantly to their children's achievement. The suggestions offered here are intended to help you engage parents in successful, long-lasting endeavors related to their children's literacy achievement.

Objective

To help a parent take an active part in his or her child's learning. To develop active cooperation between parents and teachers. To encourage students to read for pleasure during their leisure time. To promote the joy of shared reading. To encourage students to write at home.

Procedure

An excellent time to initiate the effort to involve parents is at parent-orientation evenings. The time can be used to promote and explain parent involvement in school activities. Here are some suggestions:

❖ Develop a BEAR ("Be Enthusiastic About Reading") program. The program promotes the idea of reading for enjoyment. Inform parents of the number of minutes in the suggested reading period (perhaps 20 or 30), and suggest ways that the parents and children can share books together. Remind parents that the TV or radio should be turned off during the reading periods. Finally, refer parents to the school or local library for books that their children might enjoy. The Natick Public Schools in Massachusetts, where BEAR was invented, reported nearly 100% participation among students in grades K through 5.

❖ Have a "Family Reading Contest" in which as many family members as possible are involved—mothers, fathers, uncles, aunts, grandmothers, grandfathers, and friends. While the rules may vary, there are a few basic guidelines: At school, you need to announce the contest, its purpose, and the dates for the beginning and end of the contest. Explain that family members will take turns reading to all those in the family who will listen. Ask that a record be kept at home of the number of minutes that family members spend reading and listening. The name of the book and the time (in minutes) of each reading are to be written on a 3 x 5 card, and the cards are to be sent to school once each week.

At school, the class can record the names of the books that were read. At regular intervals, winners can be announced for each class, grouped by primary and intermediate. The classes with the highest number of hours can be given a party by the Family Members' Reading Club, composed of all family members who participated.

Not every student's family is intact, and some who are, will not necessarily be interested in taking part in these family-oriented reading games. Encourage students to invite their classmates to join in the family fun so that no one need feel left out.

❖ Writing is intrinsically interesting to toddlers, and ideas come from many sources to encourage writing within the home. You can encourage writing at home in a variety of ways, and some suggestions to parents are offered here. Parents need to appreciate every early attempt at writing by praising writing efforts. Whatever has been written can be read at dinner. Writings can be displayed on the refrigerator or on a family bulletin board. Copies of the writings can be made and sent to grandparents. A scrapbook can be kept of favorite writings. Suggest to parents that they encourage their children to enter writing contests.

❖ *101 Ideas to Help Your Child Learn to Read and Write*, by Mary and Richard Behm, is a book of ideas for parents of children from cradle to school, at bedtime and on vacation, in the kitchen area, and in spite of TV. You may recommend it to parents of your students, and make use of it yourself. $6.50 per copy.

Order from:

ERIC/RCS
Indiana University
Smith Research Center, Suite 150
2805 East Tenth Street
Bloomington, IN 47408-2698
(812) 855-5847
toll-free: 1-800-759-4723

Offer parents some practical and reasonable tips for pleasurable summertime reading experiences.

- ❖ Read to children, and listen to them read every day.

- ❖ Visit the library often with children.

- ❖ Encourage the telling and retelling of stories.

- ❖ Write messages to one another—plans, activities, and schedules of the day's events.

- ❖ Encourage children to respond in writing.

- ❖ Play word games—rhyming games and riddles.

- ❖ Write words on the cards with special meaning or interest to the child.

Observation

When parents value learning and act as good role models, children absorb the idea that reading is important and pleasurable. Efforts to boost *family literacy* play a critical role in improving children's reading achievement levels. What parents do every day shows their children that literacy is, or is not, important. Encourage parents to make an effort every day to put the toys and tools of literacy in their children's hands—books, magazines, pens, pencils, crayons, and paper. Encourage children to read the print in their everyday environment—on the backs of cereal boxes, street signs, advertising, the TV screen. Read to children every day.

Comments/Notes:

Reading Parties

A Story Party

Source

ED 308 482

Paradis, Susan. *Celebrating the National Reading Initiative.* Sacramento: California State Department of Education, 1989.

Brief Description

Students of all ages enjoy dressing up for a party. Students come to the party dressed as their favorite character from a book or story they have read; then they play games in costume and in character.

Objective

To encourage interest in books by bringing children and literature together in a party setting.

Procedure

Begin by sending invitations to the guests to come to a party dressed as their favorite storybook characters, and to bring the books in which the characters are featured. Invite your students' parents, as well. From this point on, the activity can easily be adapted for students of different ages. The following are a few suggestions that will be fun for everyone:

Have games in which the characters must be identified from their costumes.

Indoors or outdoors, have a parade of the characters.

Have the students read the story (or parts of the story or a brief summary).

Plan a treasure hunt with clues that lead to a chest filled with books.

Give gift-wrapped books as party favors.

Observation

No one is ever too young or too old for the enchantment of a story party. Don't forget to offer plenty of age-appropriate food, snacks, and drinks for the party guests.

Reading Parties
Friday Night Prime Time

Source
ED 308 482

Carlin, R. Jean, Jean Dunham, & Barbara Hanno. *Celebrating the National Reading Initiative.* Sacramento: California State Department of Education, 1989.

Brief Description
Students and adults are brought together in a book-readers' slumber party to celebrate the love of reading. Participants talk, eat, sing, play, snack, see movies, listen to stories, and *read*.

Objective
To turn people into life-long readers.

Procedure
❖ Describe the plan to parents, school staff, and students. Include the purpose, arrangements, and details.

❖ Obtain permission from parents for students to participate.

❖ Ask students to come with brown-bag dinners, pillows, stuffed animals, sleeping bags, and *books*.

❖ Plan activities to engage students' interest. For example:

❖ Engage in a play involving a favorite storybook.

❖ Play word games, such as rhyming games, riddles, or concentration-type games.

❖ Have students share what they have brought to read by taking turns reading to a partner.

❖ Have students make a bookmark with a poem about sharing the love of reading.

❖ Arrange for adult supervision by parents and/or other teachers.

❖ Provide for award certificates to be distributed when the students go home.

Comment

Two possible variations of "Prime Time" for readers both begin on early Friday evening. The evening program can end just before bedtime, and everyone goes home, or it can turn into an all-night slumber party, which, the later it gets, will probably include ghost stories!

Comments/Notes:

Reading Parties

Books and Birthdays

Source

ED 308 482

Viere, Jane.
Celebrating the National Reading Initiative.
Sacramento: California State Department of Education, 1989.

Brief Description

"Books and Birthdays" is a voluntary program in which a student gives a book to the school library on his or her own birthday.

Objective

To encourage student's interest in books. To promote the voluntary giving of books. To increase the number of books on the shelves of the school library. To foster students' enjoyment of the personal reward of contributing.

Procedure

To implement "Books and Birthdays," do the following:

1. Display a collection of books that have been donated by students in the library/media center.

2. Make a special bookplate that includes the student-donor's name to be placed inside the front cover of donated books.

3. On the student's birthday, make the presentation of the bookplate to the student-donor in his or her classroom, and let the student glue the plate into the book.

4. Accompany the presentation with the singing of "Happy Birthday," and ask the class to express their appreciation to their fellow student for the gift.

5. Arrange for the student to take the book donation to the library, and place it with the existing collection of donated "birthday books."

Extension Activity

The student might be encouraged to describe briefly why that book was selected for presentation to the library.

Reading Parties

Adopt-a-Book: Phase One

Brief Description

Using the Adopt-a-Book Program, students practice democracy in action to select one book the class will promote throughout the school as their adopted book.

Objective

To provide opportunity for students to become aware of the favorite books of various individuals in the class.

To provide students in the class with the opportunity to use their "voting rights" to select one favorite book chosen by the class as its "adopted book."

Procedures

Activity 1

Explain to your students the Adopt-a-Book Program and ask who would like to try to "sell" their favorite book to the class. Students may select their own marketing methods.

Here are some sales-pitch suggestions:

- Draw a picture of an exciting/interesting portion of the book, and then tell the class about it.

- Read an exciting/interesting part of the book to the class.

- Talk the book up, trying to "sell" it as an advertising person on TV would do it.

- Develop a puppet show based on the book.

- Act out part of the book.

- Dress as the main character while reciting some dialogue from the book.

- You are not limited to these ideas.

Source

Lapsansky, Catherine and Teresa McAndrew. "Adopt a Book," *Reading Teacher* v42 n9 May 1989, p. 743.

Activity 2

Tell your students that they will be voting on the books presented.

- For each presentation write on a 5 x 8 card the following information.

  1. Title

  2. Author

  3. Classmate who presented the book

  4. Several lines of comments about the book to help you remember

  5. Based on your interest in the book, rate it from 1 to 5 (5 being highest)

Activity 3

Now the class votes on the books.

- Using a secret ballot, you will now vote for the book presented which you would like to have the class "adopt" for the Adopt-a-Book Program.

Hold a primary election in which the two books receiving the most votes are selected as candidates.

- On your 3 x 5 card, write the title of the book that was presented which is your favorite.

Next follows a run-off election, and the Adopted Book is selected from the two candidates. Follow the same voting process as in the primary election.

- Spoiled ballots will not be counted. Examples of spoiled ballots are those with misspelled titles. (Write-in candidates will be counted, but a book that gets only a single vote is unlikely to win.)

- A board of election judges will be selected to check your name off a list of eligible voters as you place your ballot in the ballot box during both the primary and the run-off election. One voter, one ballot! The judges will also count the ballots.

Reading Parties

Adopt-a-Book: Phase Two

Brief Description

Oral, written, and artistic activities to promote book adoption in your classroom and throughout the school.

Objective

To provide students with opportunities to use orality authentic writing, and artistic expression to promote their classroom's adopted book in the school-wide Adopt-a-Book Program.

Source

Lapsansky, Catherine and Teresa McAndrew. "Adopt a Book," *Reading Teacher* v42 n9 May 1989, p. 743.

Activity 1

Assist your students in writing play dialogue based on their adopted book. This provides them with real opportunities to use and develop their writing skills. Some students could design costumes for the characters in the play. The play could be presented to other classes or to parents.

Assist your students in presenting their play. They may need help with dramatic reading, voice inflection, projecting their voices, enunciation, and volume.

Activity 2

Some students may wish to write an original song. (They can make up new music or adapt a familiar tune for use with their new lyrics.) These could be shared with other classes or with parents.

Activity 3

Assist students in organizing a panel to discuss the book. Discussion might deal with the following questions:

* Who were the characters in the book?

* What were they like and what did they do?

* When did the story take place?

* Where did the story take place?

* What are the problems in the story that the characters attempt to solve?

- How do they solve the problem?

- How does the story end?

Activity 4

Some students may wish to write ads to encourage others to read the adopted book. These ads can be turned into large and colorful posters to display throughout the school.

Activity 5

Some students may want to make objects of clay, cardboard, or papier-mâché, to depict scenes, characters, or objects mentioned in the adopted book.

Activity 6

All of the students could become involved in "authentic" writing as they prepare invitations to friends and relatives asking them to come see and hear the activities associated with the Adopt-a-Book Program.

Activity 7

Have students read a section of the adopted book to a group of children in a lower grade. They will need to prepare and practice the reading prior to this experience.

Activity 8

Have students tape-record selected parts of the adopted book for sharing with students from other classes. Get in touch with your local "Books for the Blind" organization. Your students could tape-record books for other children to read who cannot see.

Comments/Notes:

Reading Parties
Battle of the Books

Source

ED 308 482

Sonntag, Ida May. *Celebrating the National Reading Initiative.* Sacramento: California State Department of Education, 1989.

Brief Description

Students are asked to answer questions about books they have read, and they earn points for their responses. Certificates are given for participation, finalists are selected, and prizes are awarded.

Objective

To increase students' interest in books. To stimulate and integrate the skills of listening, speaking, reading, and writing. To stimulate excitement about reading so that students read not only during the summer but also throughout the year.

Procedure

The "Battle of the Books" is a competition similar to television's "Quiz Bowl." The competition is structured as follows:

❖ In the spring, the elementary-level librarian visits the third-, fourth-, and fifth-grade classes to show videotapes or slides of the previous year's "Battle."

❖ At the end of the school year, each student receives a book list for summer reading of approximately 50 books suitable for students in grades three, four, and five.

❖ Parents of third-, fourth-, and fifth-grade students receive a letter describing the program and its objectives.

❖ During the summer, the students read as many of the books as they can.

❖ You get together with other teachers to draft questions about the 50 books.

❖ When school starts in the fall, students with the greatest knowledge of the books are identified through both oral and written competitions.

❖ Three finalists are selected from each grade level.

❖ Every student who has read 10 books or more receives a certificate.

❖ The books that are under discussion are placed on display for the evening of the "Battle."

❖ Librarians and teachers from other schools can be invited to serve as judges, and the district superintendent can serve as moderator.

❖ The parents and community members are invited to watch the "Battle."

❖ As the winners are announced, they receive prizes—books donated by the local bookstores.

❖ Refreshments can be served to make the event a festive and fun occasion.

Observation

This activity is similar to "Book It," a national reading incentive program sponsored by Pizza Hut, Inc. Students set their reading goals, and they are rewarded for their reading accomplishments with *free pizza*. No charge to either the schools or students! In this program, students do not compete with other students, but rather strive to meet their individual goals. "Book It" offers many suggestions to teachers on how to manage time, set goals, encourage young readers, handle reports, and organize volunteers. For more information, contact the National Director, "Book It": National Reading Incentive Program, Pizza Hut, Inc.

Comments/Notes:

Annotated Bibliography of Related Resources in the ERIC Database

Documents cited in this section provide additional ideas and activities for teaching reading strategies for the primary grades. The ED numbers for sources in *Resources In Education* are included to enable you to go directly to microfiche collections, or to order from the ERIC Document Reproduction Service (EDRS).

A Guide to Curriculum Planning in English Language Arts. Bulletin No. 6360. Wisconsin State Dept. of Public Instruction, Madison. 1986. 285 p. [ED 268 554]

Emphasizing language as a means of communication and as a learning tool, this guide to curriculum planning presents a conceptual framework for a kindergarten-through-grade-twelve language-arts program emphasizing the integration of listening, speaking, reading, writing, and media use. The content and skills sections in the guide include a statement of scope and sequence, goals and outcomes, evaluation techniques, suggestions for parents, and exemplars. Following an overview section describing the purpose of the guide, the communication approach to language arts, and the integration of the language arts, and guide discusses the following language skills: language, literature, listening, speaking, reading, writing, using media, curriculum planning, implementation and evaluation, and critical issues. (Appendices include resources, proposed guidelines for free and responsible student journalism, teacher-education program approval standards, workload and the teaching of secondary-school English, and guidelines for nonsexist uses of language.)

Archibald, Georgia, ed.; and others. *New Routes to Writing K-8.* [Revised]. Gateway Writing Project, English Department, University of Missouri, St. Louis, Missouri 63121. 1984. 200 p. [ED 260 452]

Drawing on the experiences of teachers of writing in elementary through junior high schools, the teaching strategies presented in this collection are grouped into four sections: prewriting, drafting, editing and publishing, and systems. Topics covered in the prewriting section include listening skills; thinking, speaking, and writing; interviewing; storytelling and spoken experience; perception skills; awakening the senses; and synectics. Topics covered in the drafting section include the autobiography, power writing, composite story-makers, letter writing, poetry structuring, poetry writing, writing across the curriculum, putting history in perspective with the living time line, happy holidays, and writing across the curriculum with a focus on science. Topics covered in the editing and publishing section include revising, elements of style, beginning writing and sentence lifting, peer proofreading, colorful words, playing with modifiers, teaching grammar and mechanics through writing, publishing books, and young-authors programs. Topics covered in the systems section include coping with the paperload, writing evaluation, and using computers in the writing process.

Basic Skills Resource Guide. Wisconsin State Dept. of Public Instruction, Madison. 1981. 124 p. [ED 210 259]

This directory of resources was developed to present current information about teaching techniques, instructional materials, and human resources to enhance elementary and secondary basic-skills instruction. The guides' five units cover basic skills, English and language arts, mathematics, reading, and writing. Each unit contains abstracts of selected documents, descriptions of successful local and national basic skills programs, abstracts of nonprint teacher training materials, descriptions of professional organizations, and a list of the Wisconsin Department of Public Instruction staff members who have worked in basic skills. Each listing describes the organization or product, its audience, and possible uses. The address, telephone number, and title of the contact person for each service or program cited are included.

Bolte, Anne L. "Using Themes as the Building Blocks for Learning," *Perspectives for Teachers of the Hearing Impaired,* v8 n1 p21-23 Sep-Oct 1989.

The advantages of using themes as the foundation of a language-arts program for hearing-impaired students are outlined. Methods for developing new themes, recycling old themes, having children choose their study materials, and structuring classroom activities are presented. Examples from an insect theme illustrate the approach.

Boone, Randy, ed. *Teaching Process Writing with Computers.* International Council for Computers in Education, University of Oregon, 1787 Agate Street, Eugene, Oregon 97403-9905. 1989. 162 p. [ED 325 110]

This collection of articles focuses on the use of word-processing software programs as instructional tools for students learning writing composition. Section 1 discusses the use of word processors as a composition tool within the process model of writing instruction, and includes articles entitled Should Students Use Spelling Checkers? A Recipe to Encourage Revision, Six Directions for Computer Analysis of Student Writing, Desktop Publishing: More Than Meets the Eye, and Writing with Word Processors for Remedial Students. Section 2 focuses on lesson ideas, providing detailed practical applications for using computers in the context of the process approach to teaching writing. Articles include The Computer as a Writing Tool, Creating Writing Lessons with a Word Processor, A Family Writing Project, Writing Skills with Write On! and Reading and Writing Interactive Stories. The three articles in section 3 discuss whether and how keyboarding skills should be taught. Section 4 provides reviews of 15 software packages and two articles, Creating Software for Classroom-Specific Needs, and Computer Use in the IBM 'Writing to Read' Project. Section 5 contains two additional articles that are suggested reading for those interested in computers and writing instruction. A 101-item bibliography concludes the notebook.

Carroll, Joyce Armstrong, ed. *Fusing Form with Content: A Collection of Exemplary Lessons.* 1990. 107 p. [ED 329 970]

Designed to provide examples of the art form that in teaching has been tagged the lesson cycle, this monograph contains a collection of 50 exemplary lessons that elementary and secondary English teachers have designed and that demonstrate the fusion of form and content that characterizes the art of their teaching. The monograph is divided into sections on elementary lessons, middle school lessons, secondary lessons, and mixed-level lessons.

Cheyney, Arnold B. *Teaching Reading Skills through the Newspaper.* Second Edition. Reading Aids Series; An IRA Service Bulletin. International Reading Association, 800 Barksdale Rd., PO Box 8139, Newark, Delaware 19714. 1984. 60 p. [ED 250 672]

Recognizing that newspapers are among the best supplementary instructional materials, this booklet offers suggestions for the use of newspapers for teaching or reinforcing specific reading skills. The booklet focuses on inferential and evaluative comprehension skills, and the suggestions range from how to teach students to identify main ideas and details to the development of higher order critical reading competencies. Though its major emphasis is on comprehension, the booklet devotes some attention to the reinforcement of decoding skills through the use of newspapers. Following an introduction, the first two chapters provide a rationale for using the newspaper as an instructional resource, and using it to teach reading. The remaining chapters provide suggestions in the following areas: (1) teaching a reading lesson with the newspaper, (2) developing critical readers, (3) developing vocabulary and word-identification skills, (4) developing appropriate reading rates, and (5) reading and the language arts. A list of suggested books, materials, and periodicals is appended.

Church, Susan M. "Blossoming in the Writing Community," *Language Arts*, v62 n2 p175-179 Feb. 1985. [EJ 309 889]

Describes the positive effects of peer interaction during the writing process. Illustrates by describing integration of this method in a seventh-grade classroom and how it improved the students' writing quality and attitudes.

Clague-Tweet, Claudia. *Individualized Language Arts.* 1973. 18 p. [ED 217 424]

Applicable to kindergarten through grade 12, the individualized language-arts composition program is based on actual student experiences. Once student writing samples have been plotted on a diagnostic grid, the program's manual provides teachers with specific methods for meeting students' needs. Uniting cognitive, affective, and creative learning, individualized language arts instruction moves from basic sentence construction, through paragraphing, to extended products. In sentence synthesis, students write and expand sentences from their own vocabulary. Paragraph expansion teaches them to expand their kernel sentences into paragraphs by answering when, where, why, what, or how. Framed paragraph exercises, in which students fill in blanks to complete a paragraph, help students make the transition from sentence synthesis to paragraph writing. A column of questions followed by a column of answers and a column of details provides the format for composition outlining. Advanced composition outlining, used for expository writing, employs a similar format. Expansion by modification, expansion by duplication, slotting, movability, and embedding are techniques used to improve and polish compositions.

Combs, Martha, ed. "National Reading and Language Arts Educators' Conference Yearbook." Papers from the National Reading and Language Arts Educators' Conference, 1986. 46 p. [ED 284 192]

Articles in this yearbook cover a variety of topics in the field of language-arts instruction, such as applying recent metacognition theory in reading instruction; use of journals, videotapes, and humor in the classroom; training reading teachers; and improving students' speaking and listening skills. Articles and their authors are as follows: (1) Dialogue Journals in Elementary Methods Courses (K. E. Danielson and K. H. Wendelin); (2) Achieving a Purpose for Reading: The Metacognitive Strategies of Reading Methods Students (M. F. Heller); (3) Preparing Reading Teachers to Use Research in Teaching (T. R. Schnell); (4) The Language Arts Classroom and Early Practicum Experience"Learning Techniques and Screening Devices (D. Cunningham, P. McClurg, and L. Zorko); (5) Using Videotaped Remedial Reading Instruction to Improve Teaching (W. Ramsey and D. Rocchio); (6) Building Listening Comprehension: Models for Use with Pre-Service and In-Service Teachers (B. Sperling and D. Padron); (7) Secondary Teachers' Awareness of Reading Skills (B. A. Lloyd); (8) Darwin Discovers the Teacher of Writing (R. Wilborn); (9) What's So Funny? Utilizing Characteristics of Humor to Teach Critical Reading Skills (J. E. Parks); and (10) The Language of Children's Oral and Written Stories (M. Ice).

Combs, Martha, ed. "National Reading and Language Arts Educators' Conference Yearbook." Papers from the National Reading and Language Arts Educators' Conference, 1987. 104 p. [ED 294 160]

Papers in this yearbook cover a variety of topics in the field of language-arts instruction, such as creative writing instruction, reading assessment from a Whole Language perspective, journal writing, and strategies for modifying commercial reading materials. Papers and their authors are as follows: (1) Let's Get Creative about Creative Writing in Language Arts Methods Courses (B. J. Bush); (2) Journals with a Purpose: Reading, Writing, and Thinking (K. S. Daves and M. E. Jones); (3) Making Curriculum Connections: The Centrality of Language Arts (J. K. Hultquist); (4) Relationships of Children's Stories to Reading Achievement: A Longitudinal Perspective Grades One to Six (M. Ice); (5) Reading Lesson Redesign: Strategies and Guidelines for Modifying Commercial Reading Materials (S. Macaul); (6) Multicultural Education for Reading and Language Arts Educators (L. P. Rivera); (7) The Developmental Growth of Meaning Vocabulary as Measured by Tests of Listening and Reading Vocabulary (L. V. Rodenborn); (8) Literary Gaps Invite Creative Interaction (J. Watson); (9) A Report of Attitudes of Secondary Education Students Enrolled in a Required Reading in the Content Areas Course (R. J. Weimer); (10) From Product to Process: Reading Assessment from a Whole Language Perspective (J. W. Woodley); and (11) The Low Reading Group: An Instructional and Social Dilemma (L. M. Schell).

Dunkeld, Colin; Anderson, Sandra. "The Robert Gray Journal Project. An Account of a Year-Long Journal-Writing Activity in Grades Five through Eight." Paper presented at the Annual Meeting of the National Council of Teachers of English Spring Conference, 1983. 1983. 57 p. [ED 240 592]

An Oregon school implemented a program of journal writing in grades 5 to 8 and evaluated its effects upon the language-arts curriculum and students' writing ability. Each of the 11 teachers in the project decided the amount of time to allocate to journal writing and the routines to establish, although all followed certain guidelines on confidentiality, daily feedback, and students' choice of topic. Questionnaires and interviews with the teachers at the end of the school year indicated that most attempted to respond in writing to students' journals regularly, but only two teachers responded daily; many found the task of responding to be a very heavy burden. Teachers reported obtaining useful diagnostic information from students' journals, but very few used this information for establishing instructional priorities or teaching needed skills. Over the period of nine months, every journal-writing class showed gains in spelling performance ranging from slight to almost two years; the total group also made modest gains in general writing ability, and the lower ability groups made substantial gains; the journal writing program positively influenced student scores on language usage tests.

Fleming, Margaret, Ed. "Teaching Language Creatively," *Arizona English Bulletin*, v25 n3 May 1983. [ED 276 026]

Focusing on ways to teach language intelligently and enjoyably, this journal issue contains 23 articles dealing with a variety of topics. Article titles and authors are (1) An Experiment: Immersing Students in Language (S. C. Kirby); (2) The Art of Storytaking (J. Charnock); (3) Getting Poems from the A-poetic (J. W. Broaddus); (4) Using Peer Groups to Produce a Slang Dictionary (D. W. Erickson); (5) Nuclear Doubletalk: 'Nukespeak' (S. Totten); (6) On Barberisms (J. Seely); (7) T-Shirt Communication (C. Schon and J. Ferrell); (8) Getting the Most out of Magazines (C. Pilkington); (9) A Teacher of Parody (C. Osborne); (10) Non-Sexist Language for Pedagogues (B. Wade); (11) Must Non-Sexist Language Be Ponderous? (A. Cooper); (12) Effective Speaking for Minorities (R.

DeFrank, R. Gerardi, and G. C. Benedict); (13) Qualities and Quandaries of Black English (R. Evans); (14) Something You May Need to Know about Transformational Grammar but Are Afraid to Ask (A. M. Scott); (15) Semiotics (C. Suhor); (16) Selected Activities for a Teaching Unit on Semantics (C. L. Thompson); (17) Vocabulary without Drill: Recent Trends in Pedagogy (M. H. Moran); (18) Promoting Vocabulary Development in the Content Areas (F. B. Cacha); (19) Punctuation: Phase Two, with Feeling (J. P. Beck); (20) Syllable Count and Spelling Difficulty (P. Groff); (21) Complexity in Bureaucratic Language: The Kinds of Relationships between Clauses (R. Beatty, Jr.); (22) Sentence Combining: Everything for Everybody or Something for Somebody (J. W. Ney); and (23) Dealing with the Grammar Boom: The True 'Basics' for Composition in the 80s (T. A. Lopez and B. McCrea). The journal also contains three language teaching activities; a copy of The Essentials of English, a document prepared by the National Council of Teachers of English; and a selection of haiku poetry written by students.

Franklin, Sharon and Jon Madian, eds. *The Writing Notebook: Creative Word Processing in the Classroom (November/December 1986, January/February 1987, and April/May 1987)*. Writing Notebook: Creative Word Processing in the Classroom, Editorial Offices, 2676 Emerald, Eugene, Oregon 97403. 137 p. [ED 301 883]

Produced using a Macintosh Plus and LaserWriter Printer, these journals present articles relating to word processing in the classroom. Articles and their authors for the November/December 1986 issue include: Computer Assisted Instruction: Western Europe (Owen and Irene Thomas); FrEd Writing (B. Fleury); Writing Up a Storm: An Activity for 'The Writing Workshop'; Writing with the Turtle (J. Bachman); Keyboarding"An Interview with Keith Wetzel; Keyboarding Issues and Concerns (K. Jostad and J. Madian); Show Business (S. Marcus); The Computer, Cooperative Learning & the California Writing Project (A. C. Allen); Writing Skills with 'Write On!' (J. Madian); A Scope and Sequence for Story Writing, Part 1 (J. Madian); Poetry and Cooperative Learning, Part 2; CWP on the College Campus (A. Auten); Hazelwood West Writing Lab (A. Wright); Cooperative Learning: Using the Jigsaw Technique To Learn 'AppleWorks'; Encouraging Writing in Grades 4-8; Group Role Evaluation Sheet; and A Review of 'Show Time'"MECC's New Play-Writing Tool (S. Keran). Articles and their authors for the January/February 1987 issue include: FrEd Writing: Computer Organized Writing (B. Fleury); Multischool Electronic Newspaper (C. Peck); Five Language Acquisition Strategies for Limited English and Language Disabled Students (J. Madian); Save a File (J. Piper); A Survey of Elementary Students' Attitudes toward Word Processing (K. Wetzel); A Scope and Sequence for Story Writing, Part 2 (S. Franklin and J. Madian); Writing on the College Campus (A. Auten); Rewriting–Using the Best of Both Worlds (L. Lewin); and Style Checkers: Good News and Bad News (S. Marcus). Articles and their authors for the April/May issue, focusing on writing across the curriculum, include: The AustraAlaskan Project (J. Erwin); Computers, Education, and the UK–Reflections on a Visit with Daniel Chandler (I. D. Thomas); Five Helpful Tips for Teachers Who Create Their Own Composition Materials (T. Knight); Write to Think: Teaching about Social Conflict through Imaginative Writing (B. Bigelow and L. Christiansen); Writing in the Media Center (S. Franklin); How Do I Know What They Think Until I Hear Them Say It? (S. Boyarsky); Data Bases 'R Us (S. Marcus); Connecting Literature with Writing at the Intermediate and Secondary Level (K. Jostad); The Writer Emeritus Project (L. Madian and B. Fleury); Vctr Vowelless (M. Kozikowski); Inspiring Poetry (J. Madian); The Mayflower Passenger List (D. Ardizzone); and The Writing Family Project (B. Fleury).

Gerrard, Lisa, ed. *Writing at Century's End: Essays on Computer-Assisted Composition*. McGraw-Hill Publishing Co., 13955 Manchester Rd., Manchester, Missouri 63011. 1987. 152 p. [ED 307 632]

Most of the essays in this collection originated as presentations at the University of California, Los Angeles, Conference on Computers and Writing, held in May 1985. Issues addressed in the volume range from concrete, practical considerations (such as designing classroom exercises) to political and theoretical ones (such as the instructor's status as software developer and the limits of artificial intelligence). The volume contains the following chapters: (1) Paperless Writing: Boundary Conditions and Their Implications (Edward M. Jennings); (2) Computer-Extended Audiences for Student Writers: Some Theoretical and Practical Implications (Don Payne); (3) Processing Words and Writing Instructions: Revising and Testing Word Processing Instructions in an Advanced Technical Writing Class (Erna Kelly); (4) Algorithms and Arguments: A Programming Metaphor for Composition (Diane P. Balestri); (5) Text-to-Voice Synthesis: What We Can Learn by Asking Writers to Proofread with Their Ears (Elaine O. Lees); (6) Observations on a New Remedial Language Arts Course (John C. Thoms); (7) Engineers Becoming Writers: Computers and Creativity in Technical Writing Classes (Valarie Meliotes Arms); (8) An Ethnographic Study of a High School Writing Class Using Computers: Marginal, Technically Proficient, and Productive Learners (Andrea W. Herrmann); (9) Some Ideas about Idea Processors (David N. Dobrin); (10) Expert Systems, Artificial Intelligence, and the Teaching of Writing (John E. Thiesmeyer); (11) In Search of the Writon (Michael E. Cohen); (12) The Politics of CAI and Word Processing: Some Issues for Faculty and Administrators (Deborah H. Holdstein); and (13) Computers in Thinking, Writing, and Literature (Stephen Marcus).

Hamrick, Lesanne. "Newspaper in Education Activity Book," *Temple Daily Telegram*, Texas. [1981]. 60 p. [ED 250 703]

Organized by sections of the newspaper, this booklet contains activity sheets that can be used to teach basic skills in a variety of subject areas, including language arts, reading, mathematics, social studies, and science. Designed for adaptation to most grade levels, the activity sheets allow students to use different newspaper sections to locate details, categorize, sequence, distinguish fact from opinion, locate main ideas, form sentences, find facts, think critically, solve math problems, write creatively, comprehend, organize facts, and understand consumer information.

Handbook for Planning an Effective Literature Program, Kindergarten through Grade Twelve. Publications Sales, California State Department of Education, P.O. Box 271, Sacramento, California 95802-0271. 1987. 73 p. [ED 288 194]

Intended for teachers, administrators, consultants, parents, and students who wish to review and improve elementary and secondary educational programs, this handbook provides essays discussing educational research, teaching philosophies and methods, instructional materials, and curriculum planning strategies in relation to the teaching of literature. Chapter 1 discusses the value of teaching literature for promoting aesthetic and intellectual growth, and a sense of rootedness, citizenship and ethical responsibility. Chapter 2 provides a profile of an effective literature program, covering topic and textbook selection criteria, depth of content, language use, and teaching suggestions of four grade span levels. Chapter 3 discusses the teacher's role in the program, including the teacher's responsibility to show students how to read a literary work with sensitivity and confidence, and not to provide here's-what-it-meant lectures. Chapter 4 identifies aids to an effective literature program, such as parental support, in-service teacher education, and school libraries and media centers. The handbook concludes with a checklist for assessing a school's literature program along the lines of the previous chapters and a nine-page list of selected references.

Ideas Plus: A Collection of Practical Teaching Ideas. Book Six. National Council of Teachers of English, Urbana, Illinois. 1988. 66 p. [ED 297 345]

Contributed by English teachers across the United States, the activities contained in this booklet are intended to promote the effective teaching of English and the language arts. Teaching strategies offered in the first section of the booklet are designed to stimulate language exploration with such activities as designing and carrying out independent research, using reading logs as motivators, passing along good news to parents, preparing oral book reports on how to books, and using comic strips and cartoons to teach many elements of language and literature. Activities in the second section are designed to stimulate an appreciation and understanding of literature. Specific activities in this section can be used to help students understand the distinction between plot and theme, focus their responses to what they read, link their own experiences to those of a protagonist, write poems in the voice of a particular character, understand and write character sketches, learn about Greek myths and monsters, and plan and carry out classroom projects. Activities in the third section, intended to help students improve the conception and clarity of their prose through prewriting and writing, include student self-evaluation and goal-setting, describing favorite assignments in a letter to parents, writing about world events that have touched their lives, and keeping track of multiple plot lines as they write their own interactive books.

Ideas Plus: A Collection of Practical Teaching Ideas. Book Seven. National Council of Teachers of English, Urbana, Illinois. 1989. 65 p. [ED 308 544]

Contributed by English teachers across the United States, the activities contained in this booklet are intended to promote the effective teaching of English and the language arts. Teaching strategies offered in the first section of the booklet are designed to stimulate language exploration by helping students learn to tell stories from pictures, see the personal significance in famous quotations, feel comfortable asking questions, suggest solutions to problems posed by classmates, and approach poetry through illustration, movement, and popular music. Activities in the second section are designed to stimulate an appreciation and understanding of literature. Specific activities in this section include a living literature museum, a way to introduce irony, a lighthearted pre-holiday exercise focusing on literary characters, and assignments to supplement the study of Dandelion Wine. Teaching ideas in the third section provide the means for students to learn writing from a variety of different angles and for different purposes through prewriting and writing, and include using writing for self-discovery, a descriptive-writing session based on real-estate ads, an in-house field trip, a project in which students write brochures, a way for middle-school students to pass their expertise on to incoming students, and a long-term assignment to read, evaluate, and respond to the work of a newspaper columnist.

Ideas Plus: A Collection of Practical Teaching Ideas. Book Eight. National Council of Teachers of English, 1111 Kenyon Road, Urbana, Illinois 61801. 1990. 66 p. [ED 322 528]

Contributed by English teachers across the United States, the activities contained in this booklet are intended to promote the effective teaching of English and the language arts. Teaching strategies offered in the first section of the booklet are designed to stimulate language exploration; they include activities in which students improvise dialogue and action between two characters, write and arrange readings for three voices, distinguish between fact and inference, work on discussion skills in a structured group discussion, connect concrete images with abstract concepts, and transform original fables into filmstrips. Activities in the second section are designed to stimulate an appreciation and understanding of literature; they include focusing on imagist poetry, writing ghost stories, group role playing, creating the last words of famous literary characters, staging a contemporary storytelling contest, and more. Teaching ideas in the third section provide the means for students to learn writing from a variety of different angles and for different purposes. Through this process, students become confident, effective writers. Activities include outlining a draft, using Rube Goldberg cartoons as a basis for talking and writing about cause and effect, and practicing descriptive writing by magnifying the moment.

Manarino-Leggett, Priscilla; Salomon, Phyllis A. "Cooperation vs. Competition: Techniques for Keeping Your Classroom Alive but Not Endangered." Paper presented at the Annual Meeting of the International Reading Association, 1989. 13 p. [ED 311 409]

This paper discusses cooperative learning, a technique in which students work in small heterogeneous learning groups. Following a definition of cooperative learning, the paper describes the most widely used cooperative learning methods, including Student Teams-Achievement Divisions (STAD), Teams-Games-Tournament (TGT), Jigsaw, Learning Together, and Group Investigation. The next section presents a brief review of related research. The final section offers methods and strategies applicable to the reading classroom, including Cooperative Integrated Reading and Composition (CIRC), dyads, groups of four, think-pair-share, group retellings, turn to your neighbor, reading groups, jigsaw, focus trios, drill partners, reading buddies, worksheet checkmates, homework checkers, test reviewers, composition pairs, board workers, problem solvers, computer groups, book report pairs, writing-response groups, skill teachers/concept clarifiers, group reports, summary pairs, elaborating and relating pairs, and playwrights.

Matthews, Dorothy, ed. "The English Teacher and the Arts," *Illinois English Bulletin*, v71 n2 winter 1984. [ED 239 298]

Emphasizing an aesthetic approach to language arts, this focused journal issue brings together ideas for literature and writing instruction that capitalize upon opportunities provided by all the fine arts. In general, the articles describe how field trips to art museums and theaters, film showings, in-class use of slides and pictures, and teacher-directed improvisations can supplement and enrich the English class. Specifically, the eight articles discuss (1) the connection between art and English, (2) students and cultural enrichment, (3) art and the ancient epics, (4) painting and the art of rhetoric, (5) educational drama to enhance listening skills, (6) studying the film Citizen Kane, (7) the frame-story device, and (8) 150 adolescent novels worth reading.

McLeod, Alan M., ed. "Computers in Language Arts," *Virginia English Bulletin*, v33 n2 winter 1983. 33 p. [ED 238 010]

Examining the impact of computers in language-arts instruction, this journal issue focuses on the practical classroom use of computers. The essays discuss the following topics: (1) using the personal computer to organize the language-arts curriculum; (2) computers in a writing project; (3) the potential of microcomputers for English classrooms; (4) word processors in the composition classroom; (5) the effect of word processors on reluctant or poor writers; (6) software for English instruction; (7) finding and evaluating language-arts software; (8) research supporting the use of computers in language arts; (9) teaching ideas for writing to learn; and (10) materials for a unit on censorship.

McLeod, Alan M., ed. "Evaluation and Oral Communication," *Virginia English Bulletin*, v34 n1 spring 1984. [ED 241 957]

Articles in this journal issue focus primarily on evaluation in the language arts and oral communication. Following an introduction to the two themes, the articles discuss the following: (1) pop quizzes in literature, (2) holistic scoring, (3) self-evaluation strategies in prewriting and rewriting, (4) what not to do in student/teacher conferences, (5) owning writing, (6) the Virginia Standards of Learning Program for Language Arts assessment procedures, (7) oral communication in the classroom, (8) oral communication and perceived communication, (9) researched speeches, and (10) visual literacy.

Reading and Literature in the English Language Arts Curriculum, K-12 (Draft). New York State
Education Dept., Albany. Bureau of Curriculum Development. 1988. 168 p. [ED 298 434]

As a supplement to the English Language Arts Syllabus K-12, this curriculum guide draft for reading and
literature in the English Language Arts (K-12) focuses on instruction that reflects reading as an active
meaning-centered process. The guide includes (1) a description of an integrated program in the English language
arts; (2) the characteristics and quality indicators of an effective program; (3) a description of the reading process; (4)
recommendations for nurturing the reading process in the classroom; (5) an overview of essential reading readiness
experiences; and (6) expected instructional outcomes for grades K-12. Also included is a discussion of the role of
literature in a comprehensive reading program and a chart describing the content of a balanced literature program.
The role of word identification is addressed, and finally, an evaluation section presents several informal approaches
to assessment and monitoring of student achievement in reading.

Reyhner, Jon, ed. *Teaching the Indian Child: A Bilingual/Multicultural Approach*. Bilingual
Education Program, Division of Elementary and Secondary Education, Eastern Montana
College, 1500 North 30th Street, Billings, Montana 59101-0298. 1986. 289 p. [ED 283 628]

Ideas about resources and methods especially appropriate for Indian students are presented in this book of 19
chapters by 17 authors. The bulk of the material is addressed to non-Native teachers, and teaching methods do not
require knowledge of a Native American language. The opening chapter lays out evidence of the need for improving
Native American education and describes problems contributing to poor achievement ranging from cultural
differences to irrelevant curriculum. A chapter on bilingual education presents a rationale, and it defines
components of successful programs. A discussion of self-concept and the Indian student urges teachers to expect
success, respect students and their culture, and give students responsibility. Instructional methods and selected
bibliographies are presented in chapters on reading comprehension, reading material selection, teaching Native
American literature, the whole-language approach, and English as a second language for Indian students. Specific
chapters cover social studies, science, mathematics, and physical education curriculum for Native American
students. Two chapters on Indian parents focus on children's early interactional experiences at home as they relate
to later academic achievement and recommend ways to address parental involvement. Additional chapters deal with
effective discipline for the Native American student, testing, and preserving Indian culture through oral literature.

Robinson, Brent. *Microcomputers and the Language Arts*. English, Language, and Education
Series. Open University Press, Taylor & Francis Inc., 242 Cherry St., Philadelphia,
Pennsylvania 19106-1906. 1985. 135 p. [ED 270 822]

Designed to reveal some of the strengths and weaknesses of microtechnology in the language arts, this book
suggests how and where microcomputers might have applications or implications in the language-arts curriculum.
The first chapter of the book discusses practical problems facing language-arts teachers in developing classroom
computer programs, including how to gain access to computers, how to choose hardware and software, and where to
place them for best use. The second chapter discusses computers and reading instruction, examining such areas as
beginning reading, phonics, comprehension, and the higher reading skills. The third chapter deals with computers
and writing and reviews computer use in teaching letter formation, spelling, grammar, and punctuation, and also as
a stimulus for writing. The fourth chapter covers computers and orality, touching upon computer recognition of
speech, speech synthesis, and computer-student exchanges. The book concludes with a discussion of computer use
across the curriculum.

Rosecky, Marion. *Implementing PCRP: Fact or Fiction? Communication Skills*. Pennsylvania State
Dept. of Education, Harrisburg. 1982. 16 p. [ED 214 112]

The Pennsylvania Comprehensive Reading/Communication Arts Plan (PCRP) is a language arts curriculum
providing four critical experiences that all students need in order to become competent in reading, writing, listening,
and speaking: responding to literature, sustained silent reading, oral and written composing, and investigating and
mastering language patterns. An implementation model was developed to allow maximum impact of the program, in
which the school principal models sustained silent reading and sustained writing in the classroom and designs
schedules to allow frequent teacher team meetings and inservice sessions. In providing the four critical experiences
for students, teachers focus on facilitating student learning, with the belief that teachers can positively affect the
learning of their students. Assessment of the reading and writing achievement in pilot PCRP classes at the
elementary school level indicates significant gains in both areas, and subsequent research will be conducted with
PCRP students at the secondary school level. Current results indicate positive effects for implementation of PCRP,
but the most convincing evidence that the program has made a difference for students is the teachers' growth in
reading, writing, speaking, and listening when working with their students in this approach.

Rucker, Gary H. "Regular Writing Practice—Strategies for Implementation and Evaluation." Colorado: a teacher's classroom guide, 16p. 1977. [ED 252 849]

Intended for teachers of writing in elementary and secondary school, this paper describes the Regular Writing Practice (RWP) program, which combines the philosophical and pedagogical bases of Lyman Hunt's Uninterrupted Sustained Silent Reading program with the instructional methodology of creative writing and composition. The first portion of the paper defines RWP as a supplement to language-arts programs, presents procedures for organizing an RWP program, and outlines behavioral objectives for a four-week RWP unit. The middle portion then presents a daily syllabus for the four weeks, and a list of writing activities designed for regular writing practice. The final portion of the paper presents methods for formal and informal evaluation of student writing, and RWP samples evaluated using word/T-unit counts.

Russo, Mary; Rubino, Nicholas. "Linking Reading/Language Arts and Math," *Equity and Choice*, v2 n2 p41-44 winter 1986. [EJ 330 793]

Describes how classrooms can talk the language of and write about mathematics concepts and procedures, thereby demystifying the abstraction of math and, at the same time, developing literacy skills.

Salomone, Ronald E., ed. "Teaching the Low Level Achiever," *FOCUS: Teaching English Language Arts*, v12 n2 winter 1986. [ED 270 789]

Intended for teachers of the English language arts, the articles in this issue offer suggestions and techniques for teaching the low level achiever. Titles and authors of the articles are as follows: (1) A Point to Ponder (Rachel Martin); (2) Tracking: A Self-Fulfilling Prophecy of Failure for the Low Level Achiever (James Christopher Davis); (3) Improving the Slow Learner and Inter-School Relations (Georgianna G. Clark); (4) Teaching Low-Achieving Students: Motivation for Success (M. Kay Alderman); (5) Bored Students? Try Board Games! (Miriam de la Iglesia); (6) Nurturance of Creativity (Carol Wolf); (7) Protecting the Slow Learner (Georgianna G. Clark); (8) Remedial C.A.I. (Claire Redmond); (9) College Survival: How It Works (Helen H. Pierson); (10) Not Until They Know They Do Not Know (Robert L. Wilson); (11) Individualizing Composition Instruction through CAI Commentary Programs (Leigh Holmes); (12) The Example of Gargantua: Low-Level Achiever to Model Student (Veena Kasbekar); (13) Good Hunting: A Look at the Writing of Learning Disabled Children (John Aylesworth); (14) Releasing the Reluctant Writer: Attempts at Myth-Breaking and a Friendly Assault on the Mountain of Our Own Fears (June Langford Berkley); (15) Motivational Strategies for Low Level Achievement Students (Maria Di Tommaso); (16) New Problems Need New Solutions (Susan Archer); and (17) Tutoring the Reluctant Learner (Elaine A. Vacha).

Staton, Jana. ERIC/RCS Report: Dialogue Journals, *Language Arts*, v65 n2 p198-201 Feb 1988.

Reports on dialogue journals as effective writing tasks which bridge the gap between spoken conversation and the traditional tasks of essay and report writing. Suggests that the use of dialogue journals improve classroom management and discipline, while creating an individual tutorial relationship of both an academic and personal nature.

Stoneham, Joyce Keever. "What Happens When Students Have a Real Audience?" *Journal of Teaching Writing*, v5 n2 p281-87 Fall 1986.

Discusses a children's-literature project involving a letter-writing exchange between eighth-graders and second-graders, and the students' collaboration composing short stories. Reports that the eighth-graders' reading aloud to the second-graders, and receiving suggestions for revisions, had significant audience-awareness impact on the eighth-graders' writing.

Webb, Rodman B., and others. "The Basic Skills Instructional System: A Manual for Improving the Reading and Language Arts Skills of Low Achieving Students," *Florida Educational Research and Development Council, Inc. Research Bulletin*, v17 n2 Fall 1983. [ED 246 020]

This manual presents a program of instruction, the Basic Skills Instructional System, which coordinates a number of teaching strategies into a single instructional system. Section 1 describes the organizational phase of the system: (1) teacher expectation, (2) resistance from low-achieving students, (3) avoiding confrontations, (4) management of class time, and (5) effective teaching behaviors. In the second section, the development phase of instruction is described. During this phase, new concepts or basic skills are introduced to the class. Ways in which materials are presented to ensure that all students achieve a basic understanding of what is expected of them are outlined. Section 3 is devoted to a description of the seatwork phase of instruction; the aim of this phase is to consolidate learning and to increase students' proficiency in a specific, narrow area. The fourth section provides a description of effective practices in planning, assigning, and evaluating homework. In the final section, effective techniques are outlined for reviewing critical materials so that students can retain knowledge and consolidate learned skills.

Winget, Patricia L., ed. *Integrating the Core Curriculum through Cooperative Learning. Lesson Plans for Teachers.* Resources in Special Education, 650 University Ave., Room 201, Sacramento, California 05825. 1987. 222 p. [ED 300 975]

Cooperative learning strategies are used to facilitate the integration of multicultural and multi-ability-level students into California regular education classrooms. This handbook is a sampling of innovative lesson plans using cooperative learning activities developed by teachers to incorporate the core curriculum into their instruction. Three papers introduce the cooperative learning process and give guidelines for its implementation. Twenty-seven lesson plans are then presented, with each plan outlining grade level (K-12), necessary materials, and procedures for setting the lesson, conducting the lesson, monitoring and processing, and evaluating the lesson. In the language arts/reading area, lesson plans include: Show and Tell, We'd Rather, The Goop, Brothers Grimm Fairy Tales, Jobs, Jobs, Jobs, Facts in Fives, Identifying Denial, Writing Complete Simple Sentences, and Garden Plot. Math/science lesson plans are titled Let Me Count the Ways, Gummy Bears, Beansticks, Magnets, Are You a Square? Places on the Tongue, Teddy Bear Math, Volcanoes, and Take Me to Your Liter. History/social science lesson plans cover Our United States, Exploring the Continents, Political Cartoons, Buying American, and The 1920's. A miscellaneous category includes Santa Claus, Roses Are Red, Family Squares Game, and an overview of cooperative learning for parents and teachers. Four excerpts from published works, one concerning competition and the others concerning aspects of cooperative and group learning, conclude the handbook. A list of contributors, an index by grade level, and a list of additional resource materials are appended.

All about TRIEDs
TRIED stands for Teaching Resources In the ERIC Database

Each **TRIED** volume contains at least 40 alternatives to textbook teaching. The acronym **TRIED** reflects the reliability of these hands-on, how-to instructional designs: These ideas have been **tried** and polished by other teachers, reported in the ERIC database, and now they have been redesigned to be teacher-easy and student-friendly.

A **TRIED** taps the rich collection of instructional materials and techniques collected in the ERIC database.

✦ A **TRIED** is focused on specific topics and grade levels.

✦ **TRIED**s include a wide but manageable range of practical teaching suggestions, useful and inspiring ideas, and dependable and effective classroom strategies.

✦ **TRIED**s save you time by helping you manage the information explosion, serving as your curricular introduction and guide to, or reacquaintance with, the wealth of the ERIC database, the oldest and largest information retrieval system in professional education.

SPECIAL FEATURES IN EACH TRIED

We have kept educational jargon to a minimum, wanting to put the results of the best thinking and planning into your hands in a brief, clean, interesting, easy-to-follow format. Each chapter is organized under these headings:

✦ **SOURCE**—You can look up the original document in the ERIC database for further information (if you like, but you don't have to).

✦ **BRIEF DESCRIPTION**—Outlines the focus and content of each chapter's instructional design.

✦ **OBJECTIVE**—Notes concisely students' goals.

✦ **PROCEDURES**—Details the steps to be taken.

✦ **PERSONAL OBSERVATION**—Offers helpful comments from experienced teachers.

✦ **ACTIVITIES CHART**—Cross-references classroom strategies and activities in use from chapter to chapter.

✦ **USER'S GUIDE**—Summarizes clearly the TRIED's focus.

✦ **ANNOTATED BIBLIOGRAPHY**—Provides citations and abstracts of related resources in the ERIC database.

WRITING ACROSS THE SOCIAL STUDIES CURRICULUM by Roger Sensenbaugh

Provides examples of how to connect many kinds of writing activities with lessons on important topics; a writing-across-the-curriculum approach that teaches writing and social studies simultaneously. (T01; $14.95)

TEACHING THE NOVEL by Becky Alano

Offers strategies for teaching many novels, including *To Kill a Mockingbird, The Color Purple, The Scarlet Letter,* and other oft-taught works of interest to middle-school and high-school students. An annotated bibliography leads teachers to related resources in the ERIC database. (T02; $14.95)

CRITICAL THINKING, READING, AND WRITING by Mary Morgan & Michael Shermis

Encourages reading, writing, and thinking in a critically reflective, inventive way for students at all levels. Practical classroom activities make critical thinking a feasible goal. (T03; $14.95)

WRITING EXERCISES FOR HIGH SCHOOL STUDENTS by Barbara Vultaggio

Motivates students to explore creative, descriptive, and expository writing. Introduces the young writer to audience/voice, community involvement, peer editing, collaborative writing, and other basics of good writing. (T04; $14.95)

REMEDIAL READING FOR ELEMENTARY SCHOOL STUDENTS by Carolyn Smith McGowen

Uses games and reading activities to stimulate imagination, develop reading skills, and strengthen comprehension. For grade school students with reading difficulties. (T05; $14.95)

COMPUTERS IN ENGLISH/LANGUAGE ARTS by Sharon Sorenson

Shows how to use computers to teach English and language arts at all levels. Including guidelines for language arts at all levels. Includes guidelines for word processing skills, software selection, desktop publishing, and getting set up for teachers who may be new to computers. (T06; $14.95)

READING STRATEGIES FOR THE PRIMARY GRADES by Kim & Claudia Kätz

Enables teachers to accomplish a prime goal of elementary school: making certain of basic literacy. A storehouse of clever ideas--using rhymes, pictures, and students' experiences to begin reading and writing & to build vocabulary and comprehension; story, poem, and semantic mapping; family stories, response logs, oral reading, Whole Language, and much more. (T08; $14.95)

Don't be misled by the next title: Legal and civil-rights issues affect middle-schoolers as surely as they do high-schoolers.

A HIGH-SCHOOL STUDENT'S BILL OF RIGHTS by Stephen Gottlieb

Examines a "Student's Bill of Rights." Students in school, legal minors, constitute a special class of citizens: people with the same civil rights as everyone else, but not quite. Lesson plans explore the U.S. Constitution and other bodies of law, focused on precedent- setting legal cases that have dealt with students' rights when they were contested in the school context. May be used as a whole course, a mini-course, or as supplementary activities. (T09; $14.95)

WORKING WITH SPECIAL STUDENTS IN ENGLISH/LANGUAGE ARTS by Sharon Sorenson

Many teachers worry about teaching LD and other special students "mainstreamed" into their classrooms. Sorenson takes the worry out of teaching language arts to special students. She has redesigned familiar methods to help you organize your classroom; use computers; implement cooperative learning; and teach thinking skills, reading, and writing to students with several kinds of special needs. (T10; $14.95)

CELEBRATE LITERACY! THE JOY OF READING AND WRITING by Jerry L. Johns, Susan J. Davis, June E. Barnhart, James H. Moss, & Thomas E. Wheat

The fun and games of literacy! Turn your elementary school into a reading-and-writing carnival with the principal on the roof, literacy slumber parties, book birthdays, and battles of the books. Other, somewhat more sedate, lesson plans cover the full range of language-arts skills and strategies, the use of literature, and the use of other media in literacy instruction. (T11; $14.95)

READING AND WRITING ACROSS THE HIGH-SCHOOL SCIENCE AND MATH CURRICULUM by Roger Sensenbaugh

Reading and writing alternatives to the textbook approach help the science and math teacher get the subject matter across: lessons on "writing to learn" in the sciences, cooperative teaching between the biology teacher and the English teacher, journal writing, scientific poetry writing, using writing to overcome those dreaded "word problems," and discussion of mind-stimulating scientific questions. A "Super-TRIED," this volume contains special advice on teaching science and math by simultaneously teaching reading, and on how to increase scientific understanding by generating analogies. (T12; $16.95)

TEACHING VALUES THROUGH TEACHING LITERATURE by Margaret Dodson

The literature taught in English classrooms expresses a wide range of religious, personal, moral, and social ethical values—and opinions about these values vary greatly. Many of the pieces of literature selected for lessons in this **TRIED** correspond to the literature discussed by Charles and Bernard Suhor in **Teaching Values in the Literature Classroom: A Debate in Print**. That debate and this **TRIED** are companion volumes. This volume contains many useful strategies for multicultural and environmental education. (T13; $16.95)

NB: Instructional strategies originally designed for students at one level can, by your own thoughtful effort, be readily adapted for students at another level and to your unique teaching and learning context.

Order Form

ship to:

name _____

address _____

_____

city/state/zip _____ phone (____) _____

Item No.	Qty.	Abbreviated Title	Price	Total Cost
T01		Writing across the Social Studies Curriculum	$14.95	
T02		Teaching the Novel	$14.95	
T03		Critical Thinking, Reading, and Writing	$14.95	
T04		Writing Exercises for High School Students	$14.95	
T05		Remedial Reading for Elementary School Students	$14.95	
T06		Computers in English/Language Arts	$14.95	
T07		Language Arts for Gifted Middle School Students	$14.95	
T08		Reading Strategies for the Primary Grades	$14.95	
T09		A High School Student's Bill of Rights	$14.95	
T10		Working with Special Students in English/Language Arts	$14.95	
G13		Peer Teaching and Collaborative Learning the Language Arts	$14.95	
			Subtotal	
			Plus Postage and Handling	
			TOTAL Purchase	

method of payment:

❏ check   ❏ money order   ❏ P. O. # _____   ❏ MasterCard ❏ VISA

cardholder _____   card no. _____   expiration date _____

Make checks payable to ERIC/RCS.

Send order form to:
ERIC/RCS
Indiana University
2805 E. 10th Street, Suite 150
Bloomington, IN 47408-2698
Phone: (812) 855-5847
Toll Free (800) 759-4723
Fax: (812) 855-7901

Order Subtotal	Postage and Handling
$5.00 - $10.00	$2.00
$10.01 - $25.00	$3.00
$25.01 - $50.00	$4.00
$50.01 - $75.00	$5.00
$75.01 - $100.00	$6.00
$100.01 - $125.00	$7.00
$125.01 - $150.00	$8.00
over $150.00	$9.00